"Jen Hatmaker is a fantastic storyteller, and this is one of the most important stories I can think of: the story of courage instead of fear, adventure instead of predictability, and intimate connection with God instead of routine religious to-do lists. A beautiful, funny, tender story."

SHAUNA NIEQUIST, author of *Bread and Wine* and *Cold Tangerines*

"Jen Hatmaker is a good author who writes with disarming charm and unusual honesty to deliver valuable insight into the nature of the missional lifestyle. It is especially significant to have a woman join this conversation usually monopolized by men. A great read."

ALAN HIRSCH, author of *The Forgotten Ways*; international director, Forge Mission Training Network; founder, shapevine.com

"I have a friend who says that every few hundred years, the church needs a rummage sale to get rid of the clutter and sort through the essentials. Jen Hatmaker calls us to that sort of movement, to cling to our Lover Jesus and to God's dream for the world and to interrupt everything else that gets in the way."

SHANE CLAIBORNE, author, activist, recovering sinner, www.thesimpleway.org

"Jen Hatmaker is just crazy enough to actually do things Jesus talks about in the Bible, even though it's messing up her middle-class Christian life. Warning: You will never look at your shoes (or the rest of your life) the way you used to."

KAREN LEE-THORP, coauthor of *Doing Life Together* and *Bringing the Bible to Life*

"To be interrupted by God is a beautiful thing. He grabs ahold of our faces with His tender yet firm hands, demanding that we get our eyes off ourselves and onto Him, off our mission and onto His Mission, off the mundane everyday and onto the most exciting journey of obeying Jesus' command 'Follow Me.' This book is one testimony of that beautiful interruption that will challenge the way you view your own interruptions."

MATT CARTER, senior pastor, The Austin Stone Community Church

"If you have ever wondered, 'Where is the more in my life?' *Interrupted* is for you. Jen Hatmaker's powerful message could bring the start of that new thing God will do in you."

LAWRENCE W. WILSON, past
Kind of Crazy: Living the Way Jes

JEN HATMAKER

REVISED & EXPANDED

INTER-RUPTED

WHEN JESUS WRECKS YOUR COMFORTABLE CHRISTIANITY

NAVPRESS

A NavPress resource published in alliance with Tyndale House Publishers, Inc.

NAVPRESS⬤®

NavPress is the publishing ministry of The Navigators, an international Christian organization and leader in personal spiritual development. NavPress is committed to helping people grow spiritually and enjoy lives of meaning and hope through personal and group resources that are biblically rooted, culturally relevant, and highly practical.

For more information, visit www.NavPress.com.

Interrupted: When Jesus Wrecks Your Comfortable Christianity

Copyright © 2014 by Jennifer Hatmaker. All rights reserved.

A NavPress resource published in alliance with Tyndale House Publishers, Inc.

NAVPRESS and the NAVPRESS logo are registered trademarks of NavPress, The Navigators, Colorado Springs, CO. *TYNDALE* is a registered trademark of Tyndale House Publishers, Inc. Absence of ® in connection with marks of NavPress or other parties does not indicate an absence of registration of those marks.

Cover design by Dean H. Renninger with special thanks to Jacqueline L. Nuñez

Published in association with Yates & Yates (www.yates2.com).

ISBN 978-1-63146-353-2

Printed in the United States of America

22	21	20	19	18	17	16
14	13	12	11	10	9	8

To the ordinary, extraordinary, brave, humble, generous,
Jesus-loving, people-loving folks of Austin New Church.
I can think of no group of people I'd rather do life with.

Contents

Phase Two: The Horror of Actually Changing

Phase Three: Getting Out There

Phase Four: Finding Your Tribe

Phase Five: Sent

Foreword
Brandon Hatmaker

One of my favorite movies is the 1993 film *A Perfect World*. In it, Kevin Costner plays Butch Haynes, an escaped convict from a Huntsville prison who takes a young boy hostage while stealing a car. He eventually is hunted down by Texas Ranger "Red" Garnett, played by Clint Eastwood.

Butch turns out to be a pretty good guy and takes a father-figure role with the boy. In contrast, his prison mate and escape partner, Terry, is a weasel. They're like oil and water. At one point as they're driving down the road, Terry recalls an earlier argument with Butch and mumbles under his breath, "If you ever try that . . . again . . ."

Butch interrupts, "What? . . . You were in the middle of threatening me."

"Ain't a threat," Terry replies, holding up his gun and cocking it. "It's a fact."

Butch tells the boy to take the wheel, leans over, and says, "In two seconds, I'm gonna break your nose. That's a threat." He smacks Terry straight in the face, grabs the gun from him, and as blood streams out of Terry's nostrils, Butch says, "And that's a fact."[1]

Classic.

Most of us look at change as a threat. And why not? It's foreign and jacks up what we know and like. It makes the consistent inconsistent. It typically removes comfort.

But change is not a threat. It's a fact. If we act as if change just happens upon us—surprise!—in a sudden upheaval, we miss its continuing flow and its lessons and the opportunity to keep up with it. Change is a fact of life. Throughout history, we've seen shifts in our culture, our communities, the way we think, and the way we express our faith—whether it comes from a revolution, a movement, or a ripple. Change is a reality, and we're living right in the middle of it.

The good news is that God can be found right in the middle of it as well. God does not change, but He uses change to change us. He sends us on journeys that bring us to the end of ourselves. We often feel out of control, yet if we embrace His leading, we may find ourselves on the ride of our lives.

There is a change happening in our generation. It's marked by a shift in thinking, a shift central to the missional church. And it is essential to those seeking to live on mission. This became personal for the Hatmakers in 2007, and it came with some major changes. Missiologist Rick Meigs described *missional* as "a life where 'the way of Jesus' informs and radically transforms our existence . . . where we adopt a missionary stance in relation to our culture."

He went on to reveal that "making this shift can be difficult for many . . . , but to fully appreciate what the missional church is, we must look outside of our traditional understanding of how we do church and realign ourselves with the biblical narrative."[2]

Living on mission goes far beyond the "what" and "how" of being sent; it hinges on the "who" of other people. It's about intentionally living the gospel wherever you are. This comes at great cost, but we've seen this posture become a catalyst for genuine life change.

This book is about a journey. Through it, a local church emerged and kingdom partnerships began. However, while it chronicles the birth of Austin New Church (ANC), this story mostly tells how our lives were interrupted and changed forever. On the journey we became learners again, people who are becoming. This book tells of new hearts and new minds, permission that comes from a "new command," and the discovery of an ancient way that is constantly made new again.

It was a profound moment when we realized this journey wasn't just about us or even our church. It was far bigger than that. We've found these changes happening in the hearts of believers around the world. We suspect many of you will relate.

The movie *A Perfect World* is about a boy's journey toward liberation and manhood. Butch helps him overcome being raised by an oppressive mother in a home without a father. It's a "let boys be boys, show them how to do that, and then give them permission" movie.

Our hope is that, through our story, you might identify where God is leading you, read something that helps you overcome what is holding you back, and receive permission to chase after it.

Acknowledgments

Brandon, you are a hero. Without you, there is no *Interrupted*, no story to tell, no adventure to share. If Jesus is the head of our church, you are the backbone. We're having fun together in this little life, aren't we? I love you, and I'm proud of you.

My family continues to play a larger role in our story the further we go. Standing in church last week with my brother and both sisters, all our spouses, my parents, my sister- and brother-in-law and nieces, and hearing an observer remark, "Man, there are so many of you—and you're so loud," I realized there is no me without you. You are the family of my dreams.

I've been so inspired by saints and dreamers and visionaries and renegades for the last few years. You'll never know how your lives have affected me. You are listed collectively in the Heavy Influences sections. For your obedience and courage, thank you. Thank you. Thank you. Oh, thank you. Your messages have mattered. You have an inheritance in this story.

So much love for Dennis Jeffery, Bishop Matt Thomas,

and the other leaders of the Free Methodist conference. You gave us everything we needed exactly when we needed it: leadership, encouragement, support, mentorship, and vision. We want to be just like you guys when we grow up. Thanks for welcoming us into the family.

Austin New Church, words fail me. You are the church of our heart. You are the wisest, bravest, best, most committed people I know. You have loved us and this city beyond measure, and there is no one else with whom I'd rather run this race. I sincerely love you. I am proud of you. My heart could burst.

Gratitude to the teams at NavPress and Tyndale for the double energy dedicated to this story. It is such a privilege to work with people committed to the gospel and passionate about the kingdom. Should any of you need one, I'll be your best friend.

To Curtis Yates, agent incomparable. Thank you for believing in me and for giving this story fresh wind and for taking that notebook out during our first meeting ever to communicate how *Interrupted* affected your own life. I will never forget that. You are a true brother.

Finally, I am grateful to You, Jesus, for interrupting my whole life for Your name and fame. (I'm not mad about that anymore, by the way.) I love You with every breath I breathe. May Your kingdom come in my life, my family, my church, my story.

Introduction to the Updated Edition

Reader, get in here. Come close to me and let me wrap you up in my arms and hold you tight. It's just . . . I love you. I am so happy you're here in this book with me. A handful of you have been with me for a long time. If you have any idea what "Road Trip" is, then you and I go way back. Bless it.

I'm guessing many of you found me through *7: An Experimental Mutiny Against Excess*. That was the crazy, psycho book that bonded us together, and now you follow me on Facebook and Twitter and are grateful that I overshare and have no discernable filter. Welcome. I've been this way for some time.

I travel quite a bit speaking (*speaking* is such a pompous word—I guess what I do is "teach some" or "talk about my little things" or "tell my little stories" or "cry in front of a lot of people" or "have some public rants" or "tell very borderline inappropriate anecdotes with no heed to the repercussions"). Anyhow, I can often be found at the book table at these things, as I've written a few, and I get this recurring question:

"Which of your books should I buy?"

Every time, everywhere, as recently as last week when someone posed this question, I reply:

"If you just buy one book of mine, forget that bestseller *7*. Get *Interrupted*."

This is the story of my heart, the arc I find most relevant and vital to my generation: God plucked me and my family out of complacent, comfortable, safe Christianity and dropped us into the deep end of struggle, injustice, brokenness, and a hurting humanity. Whatever used to be soft and squishy about faith gave way to a stunning urgency and painful acknowledgment of the mission at hand.

If ever there was a prequel to *7*, this is it. *Interrupted* explains the painful deconstruction that rendered my heart pliable to the message of *7* in the first place; without *Interrupted*, there couldn't have possibly been a *7*. I wasn't even exposed to those ideas; I had no concept of that layer of the gospel. I was still delivering a message entitled "How to Be a Woman of Confidence" back then, God bless us each and every one. *Interrupted* is the story before the story.

I can't articulate my thrill and gratitude about the chance to release an updated version of *Interrupted*. Of all previous books I wished had a wider readership, this is number one by a million miles. Primarily because this is the current, urgent conversation in our generation. I know that now. When I wrote *Interrupted*, I felt alone, crazy. Brandon and I thought we'd struck out as pioneers, fighting for a church that was gracious and kind again, advocating on behalf of the poor and ignored, searching for a prophetic voice in a context where we'd lost our thunder almost entirely. We weren't privy to other compatible Question Askers at the time. We were too immersed in our niche tribe, entirely cut off from the fresh spiritual wind blowing all over the place.

It has been six years since I wrote *Interrupted*, five since its release. I'll tell you this: God has enriched my life with *thousands* of like-minded people and churches since I first penned these lonely, scared words. He lifted my head, and now I see beauty, courage, vision, strength, and downright chutzpah infecting the body of Christ. I see brave pastors leading their people, entire churches faithful to their mission, ordinary believers doing the work of the kingdom so courageously that I could just lie on the ground and weep over it.

As you read *Interrupted*, don't you dare identify with the message but feel alone. Because you are so not. There is a great cloud of witnesses bearing the same weight, daring to become new wineskins for the glory of the gospel in our generation. Something beautiful and thrilling is happening. A sense of global solidarity is taking the church to incredible reaches, connecting people across culture and country and race—assuring us we belong to one another, and God loves this broken world more than we ever dared hope, and mercy shall extend further than we ever thought possible, and this life is more fulfilling than wasting away in a church pew, and we are in this race together . . .

. . . *so let's run it.*

If you are plagued with tension or discontent or a nagging sense that there must be more—that there has to be a faith somewhere that rings true and hopeful and gracious, a faith other than this mean, ugly, partisan, judgmental, self-indulgent version of Christianity, which *has* to be total bunk—then get down on your knees and thank your lucky stars. God has blessed you with this inner conflict. He isn't leaving you in complacency and boredom to check boxes and do church. He has enlisted you in the cause of your generation and is calling you forward. *You lucky thing.* You will not be left and lost, wondering what all the fuss is about, wishing things would never change.

God is doing a new thing, as He has done in every generation. We stand in that tiny spot in history in which it is our turn to experience God's fresh redemption in a new wave of believers through His supernatural ability. It is but a breath. But it is the only breath we have. God is living and active, and He still invites those with ears to hear and eyes to see into the kingdom, which Jesus explained was subversive, countercultural, radical, often hidden. The kingdom refuses to play by the rules of power politics or aggression; it refuses to bully or dominate. It whispers of embarrassing grace and thrilling insubordination, refusing to go down without fighting for mercy.

It'll cost us, dear one. I hope I make that clear in the

next few pages. The very comforts the American dream and American Christianity hold out to us are the same ones we must abandon without looking back, daring to trust that a Savior who had no place to lay His head might have the slightest idea what He was talking about. We must trust that He would never lead us astray, although you might find yourself questioning tenets that once held your sweet little life together. And that will hurt and people will probably criticize it and you might cry. I know I did.

But hear me: *You will go out in joy and be led forth in peace; the mountains and the hills will burst into song before you, and all the trees of the field will clap their hands* (Isaiah 55:12). Isaiah was right. Those trees will clap indeed. This is the stuff, good reader. *This is it.* We can follow our Jesus to every dark, scary, broken place He just insists on going, determined to heal and restore people, because He is a good Savior and we can trust Him. And as it turns out, as soon as we are willing to be the last, we actually become first. When we admit we are least, we feel like the greatest. And when we lose our lives, we find it all . . . all the love, all the life, all the thrill, all the fulfillment.

I can't believe it. Everything Jesus ever said was true.

I am so grateful you are here. I am a gentle guide, I promise. This is no expert's account, only the words of a fumbling searcher who got so much wrong before she got virtually anything right. I've never been more aware of my own poverty, foolishness, ignorance, and arrogance. As I get older, I realize I know less about the mysteries of God and more about my own tomfoolery.

Similarly, six years into church planting, I am fully aware that church is a hot mess, even the one we dreamed up in our heads that was nearly perfect (in our imagination). We are no more capable of leading some ideal church than any other pastor who came before us. Whatever arrogance we procured as staff members was quickly put to death as church planters. Though this is loosely a story that ended up as a church plant, let me be the first to tell you: Austin New Church is led by a bunch of sinners who get hundreds of things wrong and fail and struggle and let people down and have come face-to-face with our own frail humanity. Don't read one word of this narrative and think, *I have to move to Austin to be a part of this magnificent church that is nailing every principle of the gospel.* You'll be so disappointed, so fast. I can't even tell you.

This is really just a story of ordinary disciples who Jesus messed up for the kingdom. That's it. The interruption did not make us saintly or infallible or extra-incredible or above reproach. It just made us raw. It made us hungry for justice, healing, God's loving-kindness released to the nations. It made us humble, uber-aware of our selfishness—which wasn't cured by said awareness, by the way. This is a safe place for you to wrestle. You can bring all your confusion, confliction, and hypocrisy to this conversation; I will hold it all with careful hands as one who struggles with the same tensions.

It is my high privilege to journey forward with my generation. I have never felt more understood, more compatible, more connected. It will be messy and we will fumble, but we will run this race together and beg for God's kingdom to come in our generation. Faces down, heads down, we will ask for His glory to reign over our pride, over our fears, over our arrogance. May He come in power and be famous in our time, unleashing peace and salvation through His Spirit, His presence, and the willing hands of His faithful servants.

Come, Jesus. We are Yours. Have Your way with our generation.

Brandon's Take

Jen and I recently celebrated our twentieth anniversary by heading to Europe with a few of our closest friends. We took a Mediterranean cruise that landed in several Italian ports and stopped in Croatia and France prior to reaching the final destination in Barcelona, Spain. It was amazing.

It was a November trip, which landed us smack in the middle of 40- to 60-degree highs on most days. Perfect for a couple who prefers jeans, a thick hoodie, and a beanie over pretty much any other attire.

One cold morning we found ourselves strolling through the cobblestone roads of a quaint French town. We were taking in the historic buildings, the French coffee, and a bagel or two along the way when the girls "fell behind" at a local scarf shop. My friend Hugh and I were continuing down the street, staying within eyeshot, when I noticed two twentysomething homeless men sitting in a doorway ahead. One was huddled in the corner, shivering, while the other was hard at work playing a guitar, his guitar case left open for donations as he sang through the obvious pain of nearly frozen fingers.

As we approached, my mind began to recall our *Interrupted* story and how just a few years ago I would have instantly judged the young men—wondering what they did wrong, assuming they were too lazy to hold a job, and possibly speculating what liquor they would have bought with the money they collected for the day.

But today was different. I felt a genuine compassion for them. I could see they were hungry, cold, and strangers in this town. Instantly I knew I had to do something. Reaching into my pocket, I grabbed all the loose change and bills I had, gave them a nod, and put the money in the guitar case.

Although I didn't feel like I had much more to offer at the time, I felt pretty good about what I gave. I knew I didn't speak their language, didn't have a lot of time, and honestly at that point didn't know what more I could do. So I just moved on.

I noticed that Hugh had stepped into a local coffee shop to grab us a couple of cups of coffee. He exited the shop with steaming coffee in both hands . . . walked right past me . . . and approached the young men huddled around the corner.

As he knelt down and extended a cup to each of them, he stared right into their eyes . . . and they smiled. He asked their names and about their stories. In broken English they did the best they could to explain. But it didn't matter what was said; what mattered was that someone was extending something more to them than loose change or even a cup of coffee. They were being extended dignity. They were being told that they mattered enough for a thoughtful return. And that they were worth the time to just sit and enjoy their company.

As I think back on that day, I'm reminded that I'm still on a journey. That after all God has brought us through, we're still "becoming" all He desires we become. I'm still learning that the arrival is truly not the destination, that somehow the journey is the destination itself. I'm reminded that along the way, people have stories, real stories—and they are real people. In all our efforts, if we are not about people, our labors aren't really about Jesus but about us.

As Jen wrote earlier, this generation is on the right track. We're so incredibly hopeful for the church. People everywhere are asking the right questions and caring about the right things. Actions are beginning to align with dreams. So as we consider "what" we do, may we constantly be reminded "how" we do it.

Go and learn what this means: "I desire mercy, not sacrifice."
JESUS (MATTHEW 9:13)

Introduction

My parents rented our old house to murderers. This caused something of a fixation in the neighborhood.

I suppose in the name of fairness, I should clarify that the actual paying renters only harbored a murderer. But that's a detail. Because my dad is a bleeding heart and insists on seeing only the good in other people, he got talked into a shady agreement to rent our house (which we had lived in for twelve years) to two suspicious girls who had to delay their deposit until they got paid from their lucrative jobs as "entertainers." (My sister once went with Dad to their place of employment—The Lusty Lady—to collect a very late rent check, and she told him if he didn't come out in five minutes, she was calling 911.)

One lovely evening, our longtime neighbors called my dad and whispered, "Larry? There is a fleet of police cars staked around your rental house, and the officers all have guns drawn and are kicking down your front door!" While our suburban, peace-loving former neighbors cowered in their homes in fear, the Wichita police dragged a murderer out of our former home, where his "lady friends" were hiding him after his unfortunate decision to end his dealer's life.

Years later, our old neighbors still cannot get over this. It's like they're obsessed or something. We can no longer interact with them in an ordinary way:

Me: Hey, remember when we used to slide down our street when it iced over?

Neighbor: Yeah, and remember when your parents rented your house to murderers?

My dad is no longer remembered as the good-natured pastor who shoveled snow for neighbors and put on Fourth of July fireworks shows for everyone. He is now known as the slumlord who invited strippers and fugitives to cohabitate with the good people of Haysville, Kansas. Who had to replace his front door after it was kicked in by WPD.

My point is, our neighbors were so fascinated by this turn of events, they've never talked to us about anything else since. It occupies all their mental space, colors every conversation, and affects how they act. It doesn't matter that we have years of other memories together or that we were the fun family next door for so long. *Because we later rented our house to murderers.*

It is with a similar obsession that I've written *Interrupted.* There is no other message, no competing subject, nothing else but this extraordinary story God wrote into our script. This is the unplugged version of how God interrupted our typical American life and sent us in a direction we couldn't even imagine. If I seem to have tunnel vision, all I can say is that is what happens when God shouts in your face and demands entire life change. I am fixated, and the only objective as central as living out this new mandate is mobilizing others to join me.

This message is for guys and girls alike. Indeed, girls, you make up the brunt of my mission on this planet. But far more than that, you are an essential half of this discussion. *Interrupted* is not a manifesto for men or a devotional for women's issues; this is a serious conversation for the church at large. Until we are all compelled and contributing, we're settling for an anemic faith and a church that robs Christ followers of their vitality and repels the rest of the world. We don't have time to split along gender lines anymore. There is a call on our generation that must be answered by us collectively. Sequestering into our tribes is a luxury we no longer have. We are at the tipping point. Everyone has to grab an oar.

So it is with great anticipation that I enter this discussion with you. You'll find I don't peddle fluff, and when not being sarcastic, I'm dead serious about the gospel and the church in this postmodern world. This book you're holding represents the most transformational message I've ever encountered, and I've been a believer since age six, a pastor's daughter, a pastor's wife, and an author of six Christian books before I stumbled on it.

One last note on what this project is not: It is not a how-to manual. It is not an authoritative program for living missionally. It is not an expert's opinion on church trends and postmodernist thought. It is not a raging deconstruction or a soft-sell relativist approach. I am a bumbling, fumbling, searching, questioning sojourner. I have some churchy credentials, but they are irrelevant to the arc of this story. So if you're looking for a mentor or professional or someone who has already landed, put this book down and buy something by Ed Stetzer or John Piper.

However, if you're navigating the tension between your Bible and your life, or Jesus' ancient ideas and the modern wayward church, or God's kingdom on earth and reality, then welcome. Sometimes it's better to wade through murky waters with a fellow explorer than with an authority. Questions can still be investigated with another learner instead of with one who has only answers. There is much value in the struggle. I may not offer resolution, but I will humbly and gratefully enter the conversation with you. If you have looked at the church at large, the current presentation of "a good, obedient life," or the Christian effect on culture and asked, "Is this all there is?" then you're in the right place.

So then, let me tell you how my consumer, comfortable life was divinely interrupted—and perhaps yours will be too.

AUSTIN NEW CHURCH

FOUNDED MARCH 30, 2008

VISION:

WE SEE A CHURCH that equips believers and values biblical teaching. We believe that the truth of Scripture is relevant and transcends time and culture.

WE SEE A CHURCH that inspires people to learn and live the example of Christ. We believe that true inspiration will come when people see an honest image of Jesus' life and teaching.

WE SEE A CHURCH that cares passionately for the oppressed, the abandoned, the helpless, and those in spiritual, relational, emotional, and physical need. We believe it is the church's responsibility to lead this movement both in our community and throughout the world.

WE SEE A CHURCH that is driven by God's vision for unity to be bold and innovative in partnering across denominations with other churches, ministries, and organizations. We believe that together we can share the good news of Jesus Christ with a hurting world regardless of social status, ethnicity, or faith background.

WE SEE A CHURCH where people can find biblical community. We believe that the church should be the best place to build honest and encouraging relationships that speak, share, and seek to live out God's truth.

PHASE ONE:
BREAKING DOWN

We see a church that equips believers and values
biblical teaching. We believe that the truth of Scripture
is relevant and transcends time and culture.

VALUE:
Growing in understanding of God's Word.

KEY SCRIPTURE:
John 21:15-23

BLACK AND WHITE, NO?

No matter how many Februaries my son Gavin navigates in public school with the monthlong focus on Black History, he cannot grasp the concept of racism. His only exposure to the world has been his multiracial school of many colors. No amount of instruction has made any sense to him. In first grade, he came home chattering about "Martin," and deep discussion ensued. When I asked why Martin was so mistreated, Gavin could offer absolutely no explanation. So when I gently suggested that it was because of his black skin color, Gavin rolled his eyes and retorted, "Jeez, Mom. He wasn't black. He was brown." Indeed.

In February of second grade, he came home with fresh

indignation. "Mom, thank goodness we didn't live in Martin's time, because me and Dad couldn't be together!" Recalling the previous year's confusion, I asked why they'd be forced apart. "Duh! Because Dad has black hair!" The term *black* obviously applied to any old body part; the civil-rights crisis seemed fairly broad in his estimation.

When he was in fourth grade—and surely the world had ruined his innocence on this matter—I anticipated a new understanding come February. But instead, I received this weird statement: "Whew! Good thing we live in the new millennium, Mom. If we lived back in the olden days, me and Noah"—his very white, blond, blue-eyed friend up the street—"would've had to go to different schools!" I asked why he thought they'd be separated, and his answer was, "I have no idea, but for some reason no one got to go to school together back then. They just split everybody up! It was a crazy time, Mom."

Half of me is thrilled my son is so utterly naive about racism, and the other half is wondering why he cannot grasp the simple concept of skin color after six years of instruction on the issue. (This lingering confusion comes from a boy who held the E for "equal rights" on the Martin Luther King Jr. acrostic during the class poem. Touché.) Then it occurs to me that he hears these terms and studies historical events without discerning the underlying cause because he has no personal exposure to the central issue.

The facts have nothing to stick to because he misunderstands the main point.

Likewise, I still can't believe it, but I managed to attend church three times a week as a fetus, fulfill the pastor's kid role, observe every form and function of church, get swallowed whole by Christian subculture, graduate from a Baptist college, wed a pastor, serve in full-time ministry for twelve years, become a Christian author and speaker—and misunderstand the main point. I am still stunned by my capacity to spin Scripture, see what I wanted, ignore what I didn't, and use the Word to defend my life rather than define it. I now reread treasured, even memorized Scriptures and realize I never understood what they really meant. I'm a lot like my son who interpreted the civil-rights movement as a spitting contest over black hair and arbitrary school-attendance policies.

Let's back up a bit. Until two years ago, my life resembled the basic pursuit of the American dream; it just occurred in a church setting. I subscribed to the commonly agreed-upon life route: Go to college, get married, have kids, make good money, progress up the neighborhood ladder, amass beautiful things, keep our life safe and protected, raise smart children who will be wildly successful and never move back home, serve at church more than makes sense, and eventually retire in comfort. This kept me relatively safe and prosperous, just the way I liked it. Outside of tithing, we spent our money how we wanted (on ourselves), and I could live an "obedient life" without sacrificing the lifestyle I craved.

And to enlarge the church portion of that philosophy, I basically considered the church campus—Sunday morning the entry level—as the location and means to transform the average seeker into a believer. In other words, if you need something spiritual, some help, guidance, understanding, then come to us. We'll build it, and you come. Once you do, we will pour out our lives attempting to disciple you and build spiritual health into your life. My husband, Brandon, and I spent every waking moment with Christians.

We were servants of the weekend attendees.

That point of view alone kept us so busy doing church. There was a season when Brandon was gone five nights a week, leading various Bible studies and programs by his own design. We assumed this was part and parcel of the sacrifices of ministry. Still wobbly on the concept of grace, preferring to earn God's favor, we figured the pace alone meant we were on the right track. While we sincerely believe it takes all kinds, it never occurred to us to rethink, reimagine, or reconsider how we did this Christian life thing. I would have answered confidently that, yes, I was handling the gospel obediently, and I planned on continuing in this manner pretty much forever.

Looking backward, I can better identify the tension that lurked at the edges. I couldn't quite put my finger on it, but there was . . . something off for me. That something was fueled by several particulars challenging my concept of success, beginning with the nagging sensation that Brandon and I were far too consumed with worthless things. We spent an unhealthy amount of time dreaming about our next house, our next financial increase, our next level of living. Next. We were the opposite of counterculture. We were a mirror image of culture, just a churched-up version. I was vaguely aware of this, but having invited exactly zero people into our lives who might challenge this position, I easily dismissed the thought.

And yet.

There were other question marks. Like why wouldn't people commit to our church programs, despite the endless work poured into them? And why did the same people end up doing all that work? Why did 70 percent of the initial program enthusiasts drop out by the end? Why did so many leave, claiming they needed more, when we were all working eighty hours a week to meet their needs? Why couldn't I recall the last person I led to Christ? Why did I spend all my time blessing blessed people who should be on the giving side of the equation by now?

Why did I feel so dry?

READER, BEWARE: LIFE-ALTERING PRAYER AHEAD

Why did I feel so dry?

This question became the catalyst for revolution. I distinctly remember it: It was January of 2007, and I'd had two months of rest from writing and traveling. It was a sabbatical of sorts, and I was stunned to discover that I felt neither rested nor restored. I'd expected to emerge from that short season with all cylinders firing again. I had anticipated the break for months, with no events or writing deadlines in sight. Certainly it should have been the remedy to cure me of exhaustion and apathy.

I was in church that Sunday, singing a popular worship song: "My heart is dry, but still I'm singing."[1] And I realized that was it. My heart was dry. Like dry as the desert. I felt spiritually malnourished, as if I was parched. Was I just still tired? Did I mismanage my sabbatical? How did I blow this gift of rest? What more could I possibly want from this life? My existence was charmed by any standard. What was wrong with me?

I later read a perfect summation of my angst by Shane Claiborne in *The Irresistible Revolution*:

> I developed a spiritual form of [bulimia] where I did my devotions, read all the new Christian books and saw the Christian movies, and then vomited information up to friends, small groups, and pastors. But it never had the chance to digest. I had gorged myself on all the products of the Christian industrial complex but was spiritually starving to death. I was marked by an overconsumption but malnourished spiritually, suffocated by Christianity but thirsty for God.[2]

That was it, though I couldn't articulate it at the time since I was unable to determine the cause. I only knew the consequential hunger.

Let me paint the picture later that morning: I was driving home with my three kids. It was not a holy moment. It was not some silent, sacred encounter with the Spirit. There was no fasting or meditation happening. As my kids were squawking in the back, I prayed a one-line prayer simply because my Christian labor had failed me and I had no idea what else to do (and I strongly advise against this prayer unless you are quite ready for God to take you seriously and wreck your life): "God, raise up in me a holy passion."

That was it. Nothing before or after it, except me immediately telling my sons that if they didn't stop fighting, I was giving their Christmas presents away to poor kids. (And before we move on, this is just how I parent, okay? My kids get plenty of warm, fuzzy love from me, but admittedly, last week after my fifth grader opened up a fresh, sassy mouth to me, I told him to get a shovel, go to the backyard, and dig his own grave. In my house, back talk is grounds for homicide. He got the point.)

Let me tell you what I intended by that prayer: I meant, "God, give me happy feelings." I was not seriously asking for intervention that would require anything of me. Hardly. "Holy passion" meant "pull me out of this funk with Your magic happiness wand." Was that too much to ask? Can't a girl get some cheery feelings about her wonderful, prosperous life? Evidently not. Because what happened after that prayer was so monumental, so life altering, nothing will ever be the same.

It started small that very week. Like a little flicker deep within somewhere. A tiny flame that sparked and caught but had not yet engulfed my life or done any significant damage to the worldview I had constructed. Not surprisingly, it began in the Word, where God and I have always done our most serious business. He turned my undiagnosed tension into a full-blown spiritual crisis.

HOLY PASSION MEETS REMEDIAL SHEPHERD

I can't remember exactly what drew me there, but I recall being pulled to John 21, when Peter declared his love for Jesus three times after His resurrection. You should know I've studied that passage approximately forty thousand times. I've done plenty of teaching on it too, raking old Peter across the coals real good.

In fact, I remember saying, "Peter completely missed the point here." Hello, irony.

So for that weird, Holy Spirit reason that we find ourselves in a certain passage or a certain job or a certain relationship, I ended up in John 21 that January. Although I'd all but forgotten my prayer, when I turned to that chapter, an eerie sense of the Spirit fell on me like a heavy blanket. The room gave up its oxygen, and I couldn't breathe right. Suddenly, there was me, the Word, and the Spirit—and nothing else existed. Before I read one word, I knew something important was happening. It became a sacred encounter, activated by a decidedly unsacred prayer earlier that week.

> When they had finished eating, Jesus said to Simon Peter, "Simon son of John, do you love me more than these?" (verse 15)

And like it was supernaturally edited before my eyes, the verse read, "Jen, do you truly love Me more than anything?" I don't quite know how to explain Jesus' presence—intense and terrifying and gentle at the exact same time. It was an indescribable appointment.

I do, however, know how to describe my reaction to the question: shock. "Seriously? Do I really love You? Are You serious, Jesus?"

To be honest, I felt a little insulted. Kind of injured. Only because I *really* love Jesus.

Usually He would call me on some nasty trait. (Like, oh—I don't know, let me just pick something hypothetically—being stubborn as a donkey and digging my heels in and dying on every hill even when there is no logical or decent reason to care about the issue, much less be willing to die for it. Hypothetically.) These disciplinary moments I had coming. There was no shock involved. (*What?! Rolling my eyes at*

14

people isn't Christlike, Lord? I had no idea.) I can typically spot the medicine I'm about to get a mile away. In other words, I'm aware of my "troublesome areas," as my husband calls them.

But to have my love for Jesus called into question was surprising, and not in the good way. I am a big bag of trouble, no question, but I sincerely adore Jesus. I told Him as much too. With no small amount of indignation, I touted my affection for Him with all the self-righteous, sanctimonious ire I could muster. It was a compelling presentation, Oscar worthy, but it did nothing to end this train wreck of a conversation, because the next statement was worse:

> "Yes, Lord," [Peter] said, "you know that I love you." [Which was exactly what I said but with more melodrama.]
> Jesus said, "Feed my lambs." (John 21:15)

"Jen, feed My lambs." What??? I started to wonder if Jesus was just messing with me. Because I was so busy feeding the lambs, I wished some would wander off into greener pastures so there would be fewer in my flock to keep up with. If that sounds mean, sorry. But I tended some dysfunctional sheep who were prone to wander and play with wolves. They were a full-time job, and I was a mediocre shepherd at best. But Lord knows I tried hard. Or I thought He knew.

"I do feed Your lambs! *I feed them spiritually.* I herd them into Bible studies and unleash a campaign of harassment when they wander. I counsel and pray and cry and struggle with them. Everyone I know has my number and evidently isn't afraid to use it. I don't know if You've noticed, Jesus, but I write Christian books You told me to write! I travel and feed sheep all over the nation! What the heck is this?" (I was obviously feeling entitled to a little gratitude. Please bear my arrogance for a few more paragraphs, because I was about to get schooled.)

> Again Jesus said, "Simon son of John, do you love me?" (John 21:16)

"Jen, do you really love Me in a true way?" This was the moment the back of my throat tightened, and I could feel tears starting to burn. The thing is, I usually had a decent concept of how to answer Jesus:

"Will you let Me work on that sharp tongue of yours?"

"A little."

"Will you write a book for Me?" (He was artfully vague on how many.)

"Yes."

"Will you stop obsessing over predestination? I told you I'm fair."

"I'll try."

But this? "Do you really love Me?" I was at a complete loss. Because my drift is to slip into self-condemnation and doubt (I am a recovering legalist, and old habits die hard), I started to think perhaps I didn't love Jesus at all. Maybe He was exposing the worst secret I'd ever kept from myself. Was I just in this Christian thing for notoriety? For selfish reasons? For money? Oh, wait. That couldn't possibly be it. But what if the affection I felt for Christ was fake or forced?

A few minutes and several thousand tons of overreaction later, I'd decided I didn't love my husband, my kids, my family, or my friends; in fact, I was so deceived on true love that it was likely I was a sociopath. At this point, I was giving Jesus a migraine with this conversation. He was having a hard time getting through to me.

> Peter [Jen] was hurt because Jesus asked him [her] the third time, "Do you love me?" . . . "Lord, you know all things; you know that I love you."
> Jesus said, "Feed my sheep." (John 21:17)

In my utter ignorance, I thought this was about doing more of what I was already doing, or maybe just a better job of it. I was trying to figure out which sheep I was neglecting or how to be an improved shepherd to my little flock. Longer prep time for my messages? Better e-mail communication with my small-group leaders? Was this about the conversation when I told that girl to stop whining about her ex-boyfriend and grow up? Maybe that wasn't how Jesus wanted His sheep to be fed. I should definitely work on becoming more kind and precious. Basically, I was brainstorming how to improve my current performance, never imagining a whole new stage.

Nothing could have prepared me for what came next. I told Him, "I thought I was feeding Your sheep, but I'll try harder."

And from the heights of heaven, this is what I heard: "You do feed souls, but twenty-four thousand of My sheep will die today because no one fed their bellies; eighteen thousand of them are My youngest lambs, starving today in a world with plenty of food to go around. If you truly love Me, you will *feed My sheep*. My people are crumbling and dying and starving, and you're blessing blessed people and serving the saved."

I couldn't have been more floored if I'd come home to find Jesus Himself making salsa in my kitchen. I did a little checking, and those statistics were spot-on. It dawned on me that Jesus was asking me not to do more of the same but to engage a different charge altogether. He was enlisting me in the cause of my generation, the mission of God's true church.

All of a sudden, I saw my exact reflection in Peter: devoted but selfish, committed but misguided. And that is not going to be enough. It won't suffice to claim good intentions. Saying "I meant well" is not going to cut it. Not with God screaming, begging, pleading, urging us to love mercy and justice, to feed the poor and the orphaned, to care for the last and least in nearly every book of the Bible. It will not be enough one day to stand before Jesus and say, "Oh? Were You serious about all that?"

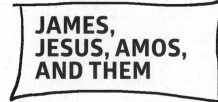

JAMES, JESUS, AMOS, AND THEM

In humble confession, I've discovered there are more than two thousand verses involving poverty, physical oppression and justice, and the redistribution of resources. Where had I been for my entire adult life? What Bible was I reading? How had I interpreted those passages as God's intention to bless me a little more than I had already been blessed? Oppression? Oh, I knew oppression! I work for the church, for Pete's sake. Lord, have mercy.

Jesus' brother got in on the action too:

Listen, my dear brothers and sisters: Has not God chosen those who are poor in the eyes of the world to be rich in faith and to inherit the kingdom

he promised those who love him? But you have
dishonored the poor. . . .

If you really keep the royal law found in
Scripture, "Love your neighbor as yourself," you
are doing right. . . . What good is it, my brothers
and sisters, if a man claims to have faith but has no
deeds? Can such faith save him? *Suppose a brother or
a sister is without clothes and daily food. If one of you
says to them, "Go in peace; keep warm and well fed,"
but does nothing about their physical needs, what good
is it?* (James 2:5-6, 8, 14-16)

Hey, here's something crazy: In the Word, poverty, wid-
ows, hunger—these are not metaphors. There are billions of
lambs that literally need to be fed. With food.

So James is totally in my head. And Jesus. And all the
prophets. Oh, and the patriarchs. God, too. Plus the disciples.
And whoever wrote Hebrews. Because the thing is, they are
all saying the same thing, and I've been either a narcissis-
tic moron or a blind fool my entire life because I managed
to miss the point. For all my self-proclaimed love of God's
Word, what I really loved were the parts that worked for me.
For my good. For my blessings. The sections that made for
a great outline or fit a funny story I had in the queue. The
themes I knew my listeners wanted to hear. Who wants their
conference speaker to worry them with poverty when she
could bring a message titled "Managing the Home"? (I actually gave that talk. Jesus, give my listeners strength.)

The night before he was assassinated, Dr. Martin Luther King Jr. proclaimed,

> Who is it that is supposed to articulate the longings and aspirations of the people more than the preacher? Somehow the preacher must have a kind of fire shut up in his bones, and whenever injustice is around he must tell it. Somehow the preacher must be an Amos, who said, "When God speaks, who can but prophesy?" Again with Amos, "Let justice roll down like waters and righteousness like a mighty stream." Somehow the preacher must say with Jesus, "The spirit of the Lord is upon me, because He hath anointed me, and He's anointed me to deal with the problems of the poor."[1]

So what are the problems of the poor?

WARNING: THE PROBLEMS ARE BAD

This stage began with necessary exposure and education, and shifting the problems of the poor from a fuzzy, distant idea to a clarified, realistic awareness was a little traumatizing. Jeffrey Sachs explained in *The End of Poverty*,

> If economic development is a ladder with higher rungs representing steps up the path to economic well-being, there are roughly one billion people around the world, one sixth of humanity, who [are] . . . too ill, hungry, or destitute even to get a foot on the first rung of the developmental ladder. These people are the "poorest of the poor," or the "extreme poor" of the planet.[1]

This bottom layer of destitution will never be alleviated without intervention. The majority of the extreme poor are caught in a poverty trap, unable to escape from deprivation because of disease, physical isolation, climate stress, environmental degradation, and poverty itself. Lifesaving solutions exist, and most are inexpensive and available—but these families and their governments lack the financial means to obtain them.

Sachs continued,

> A few rungs up the developmental ladder is the
> upper end of the low-income world, where roughly
> another 1.5 billion people . . . are "the poor." They
> live above mere subsistence. Although daily survival
> is pretty much assured, they struggle in the cities
> and countryside to make ends meet. Death is not
> at their door, but chronic financial hardship and a
> lack of basic amenities such as safe drinking water
> and functioning latrines are part of their daily lives.
> Together, the extreme poor (around 1 billion) and
> the poor (another 1.5 billion) make up roughly
> 40 percent of humanity.[2]

Because these numbers are hard to wrap our minds around, let's make this crisis more tangible. I submit the following not to shame the rich West but to offer perspective. If you've lived abroad or have global exposure, this will be familiar. But if you've never thought critically about swallowing the American pill, please come with me and step outside the construct of Western thought. These are pretty agreed-upon statistics, and if I encountered a discrepancy in the research, I went with the more conservative number:

- Of the six billion people on planet Earth, about 1.2 billion live on twenty-three cents a day.[3]
- Half the world lives on less than two dollars and fifty cents a day.[4]
- The wealthiest one billion people average seventy dollars a day. (This places you and me in the upper, upper, upper percentages of the global population.)
  - If you make thirty-five thousand dollars annually, you are in the top 4 percent.
  - If you make fifty thousand dollars annually, the top 1 percent.[5]
- Someone dies of hunger every 3.6 seconds.[6]
- Last year twenty-two million people died of preventable diseases; ten million were children.[7]
- Twenty-seven million children and adults are trapped in slavery (sex slaves, labor slaves, child soldiers, and child slaves) because of economic crisis.[8] More slaves exist today than *ever before in human history*.
- More than 143 million children in the developing world have been orphaned (equivalent to more than half the population of the United States).[9]

- In the last hour:
  - Over 1,625 children were forced to the streets by the death or abuse of an adult.
  - Over 115 children became prostitutes.
  - Over 66 children under the age of fifteen were infected with HIV.[10]
- Roughly 1 billion people in the world do not have suitable housing, and 100 million are entirely homeless.[11]

Clearly, these are the problems of the poor. When God shook Israel awake from her violent slumber, He said, "Now this was the sin of your sister Sodom: She and her daughters were *arrogant, overfed and unconcerned*; they did not help the poor and needy" (Ezekiel 16:49, emphasis added). I humbly propose that God is calling rich believers in America (which is all of us) to the same reform. Again, with perspective— not guilt-mongering—as our singular motive, let's try to impartially observe the global economic canvas on display for the rest of the world:

- 780 million people lack basic water sanitation, which results in disease, death, wastewater for drinking, and loss of immunity.[12]
  - Americans consume twenty-six billion liters of bottled water a year.[13]
- We spend more annually on trash bags than nearly half the world spends on all goods combined.[14]

- Fifty-seven million children worldwide work every day instead of go to school.[15]
- Four out of five Americans are high school graduates.[16]
- The poorest one-fifth of the world owns 1 percent of the world's cars.
  - The richest one-fifth of the world owns 87 percent of the world's cars.[17]
- Roughly forty million people (the equivalent of about seven Jewish Holocausts) die annually from starvation, disease, and malnutrition.
  - 69 percent of US adults and 18 percent of children and adolescents are overweight or obese.[18]
- The United States makes up 4.5 percent of the global population, but we consume 20 percent of the world's oil.[19]
  - We consume twenty million barrels of oil a day;[20] next is China at just 9.2 million a day.[21]
  - 20 percent of our imported oil comes from the Persian Gulf. We put military bases on two of their three Islamic holy sites, and when criticized, one US official replied that the United States "must have free access to the region's resources."[22]
- When a group of leaders from 172 developed nations begged US government leaders to explore intervention options for environmental standards via the Earth Summit, President George H. W. Bush said, "The American way of life is not negotiable."[23]

Brand America is in trouble. I ask you humbly: can you see why when Americans say *democracy*, the world hears *greed*? What seems like basic freedom to us sounds like vast consumption to everyone else. The tongue-in-cheek "First World Problems" we joke about while lamenting, "I just used my last Pandora skip for the hour, *and the next song is even worse*!" is part and parcel of the image we are outsourcing to a suffering planet. We appear indulged and entitled and oblivious to global crises and our contribution to the disparity.

"NAME IT AND CLAIM IT" (AND I'LL SHAME IT)

This is more than a public-relations crisis for Team USA. As much as we know differently, the world believes we are a Christian nation. Ask around the planet, and you'll hear that we are rich Christians, all. So they simply cannot square how much money we have with how we spend it. Global church leaders are dumbfounded at our excess while their people are dying and starving, especially when so many leading spiritual voices here are proclaiming the prosperity gospel:

- "I preach that anybody can improve their lives. I think God wants us to be prosperous. I think he wants us to be happy. To me, you need to have money to pay your bills. I think God wants us to send our kids to college."—Joel Osteen, pastor of the biggest megachurch in America[1]

- "Prosperity is a major requirement in the establishment of God's will," and "God's will for His people today is abundance."—Kenneth and Gloria Copeland, televangelists in the Prosperity Gospel movement[2]

- "Now, last night we began to deal with the relationship between peace and prosperity . . . and we'll look at it again tonight. It says, 'my soul is far from prosperity.' Why? . . . 'My soul's far from peace because I forgot prosperity.' We established last night that *you are not whole until you get your money.*"— Creflo Dollar, founder of World Changers Church International[3] (Crazy Guy Alert.)

How do these leaders explain the economic situation of believers in the developing world? Or for the impoverished demographics in America? God doesn't care about struggling people's prosperity, only ours? God wants well-heeled American kids to go to college, but He's okay with sixty-five million orphans panhandling in Asia? God wants to give us nice things but doesn't feel like helping Africans with things like food and water? It's ridiculous. Or as Rick Warren, pastor of the fourth-largest megachurch in America, said,

This idea that God wants everybody to be wealthy? There is a word for that: baloney. It's creating a false idol. You don't measure your self-worth by your net worth. I can show you millions of faithful followers of Christ who live in poverty. Why isn't everyone in the church a millionaire?[4]

The world knows about our Jesus. They know about His poverty and love of the underdog. They know He told His followers to care for the poor and to share. They've heard about His radical economic theories and revolutionary redistribution concepts. They might not understand the nuances of His divinity or the various shades of His theology, but they know He was a friend of the oppressed.

So Americans living in excess beyond imagination while the world cries out for intervention is an unbearable tension and utterly misrepresents God's kingdom. While the richest people in the world pray to get richer, the rest of the world endures unimaginable suffering with their faces pressed to the window of our prosperity . . . and we carry on, oblivious. As Gandhi once famously said, "I like your Christ, I do not like your Christians. Your Christians are so unlike your Christ."

And, frankly, our silence threatens not only the world's poor but our own security. Colin Powell wisely observed, "We cannot win the war on terrorism until we confront the social and political roots of poverty."[5] (Solomon agreed in Proverbs 29:4: "By *justice* a king gives a country stability" [emphasis added].) It is easy to see how, when people are impoverished and desperate yet know we have everything they need in the cushions of our couches, a tyrannical leader can influence them toward our harm: "I'll feed you and get you a gun. We'll fight greedy America." We'll never be safe while we ignore the extreme poverty of everyone else. Some kill by violence, but we've let them suffer and die by neglect.

I can hear Jesus' crazy words making sense: "Love your enemies" (Luke 6:27). It's hard to hate a rich country that is feeding you, advocating for your orphans, building schools in your villages, championing your human rights, and empowering your leaders. It's difficult to dismiss the idea of a redeeming Christ when His followers are pouring their lives out. It's tough to hate the Christian church when her members refuse to sit idly on their piles of luxuries while the rest of the world suffers.

GIVING THE GOOD STATS SOME PLAY

I had a parent/teacher conference with my son Caleb's first-grade teacher. Anytime my kids talk to an adult without me there to monitor the discussion, I'm nervous, and Caleb's teacher gave me plenty of ammunition to support that paranoia. Evidently, when she asked the kids in her class what they wanted to be when they grew up, Caleb raised his little hand eagerly and replied, "When I grow up, I want to be a missionary and tell people about God, even though my mom told me all missionaries get murdered."

Note to self: When talking to my kids about being grateful for the freedom to go to church whenever and however we want, exercise caution when elaborating on how some people in other countries can't go to church and—wait for it—even die for their faith, because the six-year-old will tweak that factoid and make me sound like a dimwit during the retelling.

That said, I realize I've been similarly unbalanced when dealing with global relief work by the United States. There is always another side of the story. Not all missionaries are murdered, and not all Americans are ignorant, consumerist fat cats. American philanthropy is legendary, and private giving makes up the brunt of it. The Giving USA Foundation reported that charitable giving in 2011 reached $278 billion, with $246 billion given privately (as opposed to government assistance).[1] Much of that charity was domestic, but certainly billions of American dollars reach around the globe annually.

I also appreciate that thousands of churches are faithfully focused on missions work and foreign relief efforts. Of the $246 billion given to charity in 2011, almost 30 percent of that went to churches, and many use a large portion of those tithes not just for costly overhead and salaries but for poverty alleviation.

I've witnessed people giving so generously of their time, their love, their money that I've been rendered speechless. Please don't hear me say that America stinks and all her citizens are narcissists. It's just that most of us have no concept of our own prosperity. Nor do we have an accurate understanding of the plight of the rest of the world. Our perspective is limited, and our church culture is so consumer oriented that we're blinded to our responsibility to see God's kingdom come to "all nations," as He was so fond of saying in His Word.

A couple recently left our new church, citing our vision to be missional and socially active: "We believe what you're doing is right, but we're just not motivated by it. I need my pastor to deal with me." I had a good friend send an e-mail saying, "You're being so unfair. America gives and gives and gives, and you're making us feel guilty for what we have." (And yes, while we rank number one in charitable giving internationally, we are *5th to last* in percentage of Gross National Income donated, at .2 percent, decidedly under the GNI United Nations Official Development Assistance target of .7 percent. Sweden is the Big Giver at 1.02 percent of their GNI.[2] Well played, Swedes! Meatballs and lingonberry jam for everyone!) I gently asked, "Let's set aside what America is or is not giving and answer for ourselves: What are *you* doing? What am *I* doing?"

Silence.

And that's really where we are. We stand at the intersection of extreme privilege and extreme poverty, and we have a question to answer: Do I care? Am I moved by the suffering of all nations? Am I even concerned about the homeless guy on the corner? Am I willing to take the Bible at face value and concur that God is obsessed with social justice? I won't answer one day for how the US government spent billions of dollars on the war in Iraq ($816 billion and counting, when $9 billion would solve the planet's water crisis[3]), nor will I get the credit for the general philanthropy of others.

It will come down to what *I* did. What *you* did.

What we did together.

Of course, all I can do is make the tiniest ripple in the ocean. That's about all you're good for too. But it's foolish to become paralyzed by the scope of suffering or discouraged by the limit of our reach. Though it's impossible to quantify, it's estimated that roughly 2.1 billion people—about one-third of the planet—identify themselves as Christians. Let's just halve that number to be safe. Imagine if 1 billion believers, many of them with every necessary resource, obediently decided to love this broken world as they love themselves. Then, indeed, we would become "good news to the poor" (Luke 4:18).

Alone, we can affect a few.

But together, we can change the world.

Let no one be discouraged by the belief there is
nothing one man [or one woman] can do against the
enormous array of the world's ills—against misery
and ignorance, injustice and violence. . . . Few will
have the greatness to bend history itself; but each
of us can work to change a small portion of events,
and in the total of all those acts will be written the
history of this generation. . . .

It is from the numberless diverse acts of courage
and belief that human history is shaped. Each time
a man [or woman] stands up for an ideal, or acts
to improve the lot of others, or strikes out against

injustice, he [or she] sends a tiny ripple of hope, and crossing each other from a million different centers of energy and daring, those ripples build a current which can sweep down the mightiest walls of oppression and resistance.—Robert F. Kennedy[4]

The righteous care about justice for the poor.—God[5]

Heavy Influences—Phase One

- *The Irresistible Revolution* by Shane Claiborne
- "Calling All Peacemakers" sermon series by Rob Bell
- *The End of Poverty* by Jeffrey D. Sachs
- *Submerge* by John B. Hayes
- *Speaking My Mind* by Tony Campolo
- *The Secret Message of Jesus* by Brian McLaren
- *Infidel* by Ayaan Hirsi Ali
- *A Long Way Gone* by Ishmael Beah
- The Miracle Foundation

Brandon's Take

In case anyone is wondering, I was completely oblivious to Jen's inner tension during this season. It's sad, especially for a pastor, when your wife has to go through something so deep alone. But looking back, I see how divine God's timing and order really were. While Jen would have been supportive if this had all started in me, this wasn't something a wife should be dragged into; she needed to be all in. Even more, we needed to be in this together, and if it took God moving Jen first, then so be it.

In fact, ten years ago I began noticing a pattern in men. Especially pastors. We tend to make major life decisions, drag our wives along—criticizing their lack of faith or praising their submission—and expect them to just toe the company line. The result?

When things go well, we're the heroes. But when things go south, we aren't emotionally in it together, and it becomes us against them. We end up defending our church, our work hours, the toll on our family—and we're all alone. Many pastors' wives feel as though the church is the "other woman." It is beyond unhealthy when a husband is emotionally alone in ministry without the backing of his bride. In a survey of pastors' wives administered by Focus on the Family, 88 percent of all respondents answered yes to the question "Have you ever experienced periods of depression?"[1] That's not a good statistic. (I would imagine many corporate wives feel the same.)

So fifteen years ago I began to pray, "God, don't move in me unless You move in Jen. In fact, for the big things, move in her heart first." I believe that God wants us to see Him clearly, so I literally asked Him to affirm His hand through Jen in all things big, that we might be in unity. I begged Him, "God, don't call me if You don't call my wife, too. If You don't, I'm not going. I'm just gonna read that as if I'm missing it."

It's a biblical concept, really. Sound familiar? "'For this reason a man will leave his father and mother and be united to his wife, and the two will become one flesh.' So they are no longer two, but one flesh" (Mark 10:7-8). If we are to be anything, it's one.

God uses women as the catalyst in much of His work. Look in the Scriptures. Look in our churches. It's the women who seem sensitive to God's Spirit; their intimacy with God is heightened to a level few men experience. So if you trust the faith of your wife, why not simply ask God to speak in unison to you both? (That's a two-way street. Ladies, you hear me?)

Talk about a life of mutual respect and love.

Easier said than done? Sometimes. Jen started reading books and asking me stuff like, "What if we're missing out on this whole thing?" And all along I'm thinking, *Are you kidding me? We're pretty much "all in" here. I oversee the spiritual development of a great church that baptized more than four hundred people last year. We've arrived at the place we always wanted to be! My staff, my position, my church—not only do I love what I'm doing, but I love how I'm doing it. And now you're wondering if we need to change every motivation and method that got us here?*

At this point, it never crossed my mind that a move was on our horizon. But I did know that this was serious for Jen. So I ignored her. And promised I'd read those books and listen to those sermons . . . someday.

However, I did suspect we were entering a new season. God was moving in Jen. He was pumping a new passion and a fresh wind into her faith that I was privately jealous of. I knew that if I was faithful to the deal I made with God years ago, it would lead me to a dangerous prayer of my own, which I finally offered later that spring: "God, if You're really in this, show me, too."

PHASE TWO:
THE HORROR
OF ACTUALLY
CHANGING

We see a church that inspires people to learn and live the example of Christ. We believe that true inspiration will come when people see an honest image of Jesus' life and teaching.

VALUE:
*The greatest command is to
love God and love others.*

KEY SCRIPTURE:
Luke 22:14-27

THE TROUBLE
WITH BANANAS

I have a tendency to select friends who are—je ne sais quoi?—firecrackers. Because my giant personality can cannibalize a Precious Person, most of my friends are loud and insensitive, just like me. Consequently, they provide a steady stream of material, as they are constantly in verbal scrapes because of their inability to back down once they've locked into a confrontation. (Do you like my choice of pronouns? "They" need our prayers, obviously.) Case in point: My friend Christi recently described a battle between her and her usually mild-mannered hubby, Brett. Typically, he is the yin to her yang, the cool, bubbling stream to her wild class-5 rapids. Brett is normally so calm and soothing that I want to lay my head in his lap and take a nap. But even Jesus went postal once in a while, so Brett is entitled to the occasional hotheaded moment like the rest of us.

The backstory to the meltdown involved Brett doing missions work in Mexico for three days, only to get home, repack, and immediately leave for a four-day business trip. After a week of round-the-clock labor, he was physically and emotionally spent. Of course, that left Christi to single-handedly care for their impetuous three-year-old daughter and five-month-old son for seven days without a break.

Recipe for disaster, anyone?

In a burst of good discernment, Brett let Christi sleep in his first morning back. So she walked downstairs to find the kids playing while Brett read the paper in the kitchen. The night before, she'd used half a banana—and now she observed a new banana cut in half, while the half she'd left sat unused on the counter.

Christi: Did you cut that new banana in half?
Brett: Yes.
Christi: What did you do with it?
Brett: I fed the baby, of course!
Christi: What do you mean "of course"?! You haven't fed that boy breakfast once in the 146 days he has lived on this planet! I would no more assume that you fed him half a banana than I'd expect to discover you breast-fed him too! And why didn't you use the banana that was already cut? How could you possibly miss the banana half sitting three millimeters away from the whole one?!

Brett: I just cut the first banana I saw!

Christi: We can't just be cutting new bananas all the time when there are perfectly good halves going to waste! We're not millionaires! Think, Brett, think!

[*Insert the sound of Brett's psyche snapping like a dry twig.*]

Brett: (*Tossing some change from his pocket on the counter*) Here you go. There's eighty-nine cents. Go buy yourself a whole new bunch of bananas! Sure hope we can still pay the mortgage! Hey, kids—guess what? If you drop a piece of banana on the carpet, you're eating it, dog hair and all! Because we don't waste an ounce of banana in this house! We *steward* our bananas! To whom much has been given, much will be required. We've been given a load of bananas, and *we will be found faithful with our bananas*! (*Shoving the aforementioned half a banana into his mouth in one bite*) I am eternally grateful for the nourishment of this banana! Daily potassium? Check! And, surprisingly, *a full day's worth of vitamin C*! Waste not, want not, *not in this house*!

It was, in short, the banana that broke the camel's back.

The trouble with humans is that when we are already idling high, it doesn't take but the slightest provocation for the banana to really hit the fan. When we're burdened with fatigue or frustration, things often get worse before they get better. Sometimes we don't gain clarity on our condition until we suffer a personal Armageddon over produce.

This is precisely how the trajectory of my story went too. I was troubled with fresh conviction and shocking ignorance, and the racket in my head grew much worse before it got better. It's one thing to acknowledge a different worldview; it's another thing to absorb it. The next season was marked by me thrashing around, ranting and raving, and generally freaking out as the spiritual tension caught up with me and exposed the true condition of my heart.

I was frozen, attempting to get my head around the idea that I'd missed something so central. I was sitting on the proverbial curb by the wreck God had engineered, trying to catch my breath. But that was less chaotic than the subsequent direction change. Switching gears was on par with teaching my parents to text message.

Thus began a period of reorienting my mind in the restorative mission of Christ. I was convinced of the need to change my mind, but what came next was actually changing my mind, and I don't envy God that task. (I once told my husband regarding an impending move, "I'm not even going to pray about that." This was what Jesus was up against.)

TEACHING
AN OLD DOG
NEW TRICKS

As I mentioned before, God does His heaviest spiritual lifting with me in the Word. So back at the drawing board, a theme began to lift. I began noticing the liberal use of the word *new*, particularly once Jesus hit the scene. Since that concept was hitting close to home, I dug in:

- New wine has to be poured into new wineskins.[1]
- The kingdom of heaven is a storehouse of not just old treasures but new ones too.[2]
- Jesus rolled out a whole new teaching.[3]
- We have a new and different life linked to the way Jesus lived and died.[4]

- We're supposed to be serving in a new way, the way of the Spirit.[5]
- All our rules mean nothing; the only thing that matters is being a new kind of human.[6]
- Part of our salvation is having a new attitude about things.[7]

I realize these Scriptures might sound rote. Certainly, I once had an explanation for each that fit the way I was living. I was one click away from saying, "Blah, blah, blah," so familiar were those words—white noise in the Bible almost. But as I mentioned earlier, the Bible took on a new dimension for me, and I discovered significance in verses I'd read with near boredom.

The concept of "new" began to trouble me for the first time. Let's go old-school and peek at the actual definition: "Other than the former or the old; different and better."[8] Well, because I came to Christ at age six and was a citizen of Christian culture my entire life, I didn't have a great concept of "the old me." The old me before salvation was in kindergarten, learning how to sort and sequence, so I went broader in terms of old, meaning a life ungoverned by Jesus' principles. The kind of life Jesus introduced was new; everything outside of that was old.

Perhaps the synonym that most grieved me was *different*. Because, sure, parts of my life were different from your average Westerner's, but not really. I went to church way more than a normal human would or should, but I still had too much debt, too much pride, too much self-absorption, same as everyone. I lived for me and mine. Outside of my spiritual titles—pastor's wife, Bible teacher, Christian author and speaker—there were no radical lifestyle distinctions that would cause anyone to say, "Wow, you live a really different life."

I realized I was completely normal.

But my Savior was the most un-normal guy ever.

And it was *His* un-normal ideas that made everything new.

Truly, Jesus never fit in. He was never the cool guy. He was always wrecking everyone's life. I'm positive the disciples sat on pins and needles when Jesus talked to a crowd, worried what crazy thing He might say next. (Pretty talk: "I am the bread of life." Minutes later: "Unless you eat the flesh of the Son of Man and drink his blood, you have no life in you."[9] *Dang it!*)

But it wasn't just what He said; it was what He did. It was who He spent time with, who He talked to, who He argued with—to say nothing of His very unaffluent life. If we took Jesus' famous teachings away and just focused on the way He lived, He would still be radical. Which, of course, I've heard, but somehow I was content letting Jesus do the messy work. I would just talk about it. Or I made it fit, inventing a way to merge it with my normal context. Sure, He hung out with lepers, but we don't really have a leprosy epidemic anymore, so I'll just be kind to customer service reps and telemarketers, which is about the same sacrifice . . . am I right?

DESIRING, DOING, AND REMEMBERING

God began the hard work of closing the normal/un-normal gap in me through the story of Jesus' Passover meal the night before His crucifixion. The familiar implication of this account gave way to something deeper and far more profound. It was, as Jesus often told my ancestors (the Pharisees), like blinders fell off my eyes.

> They prepared the Passover.
> When the hour came, Jesus and his apostles reclined at the table. And he said to them, "I have eagerly desired to eat this Passover with you before I suffer. For I tell you, I will not eat it again

until it finds fulfillment in the kingdom of God."
(Luke 22:13-16)

Jesus was seriously making a point with that statement. In Greek, He literally said, "I have desired with desire to eat this Passover with you." (It calls to mind Ben Stiller's character in *Dodgeball*: "Nobody makes me bleed my own blood."[1]) Jesus was underscoring His great anticipation for this moment. He had been waiting, and this was it. This was big. This was monumental. He would become living theology to change the course of history. It was time to make old things brand-spanking new.

> He took bread, gave thanks and broke it, and gave it to them, saying, "This is my body given for you; do this in remembrance of me."
> In the same way, after the supper he took the cup, saying, "This cup is the new covenant in my blood, which is poured out for you." (Luke 22:19-20)

This was a radical moment for the disciples. Jesus was redefining a Jewish ritual with a 1,500-year history. In a culture that revered ancient feasts and festivals *as is*, Jesus was transforming the untransformable. It's hard to imagine how bizarre this sounded to the disciples, which might help us understand how they possibly got into an argument about Top Disciple three minutes later.

"This is My body. This is My blood." Jesus didn't just

host and serve the meal; He became the meal. He was the sacrificial Lamb, broken for the redemption of humanity, forever our feast and sustenance. He was the sacrifice and offering, the High Priest and reigning King. He alone understood the necessary tension between His submission and dominion. The Lamb went willingly, embracing sacrifice.

"The Son of Man will go as it has been decreed."[2]
"No one takes [my life] from me."[3]
"I lay it down of my own accord."[4]

That's right, Judas. You were but a pawn in the sovereign plan of the Most High. The singular reason you were allowed near Jesus in betrayal is because this was your pre-ordained hour of darkness—not before or after. The angry mob didn't "catch" Jesus. The high priest didn't decide His fate. The false witnesses, Herod, Pilate, soldiers—none took His life. Jesus had eluded death countless times before the cross.

He laid His own life down at the appointed time—not under coercion or constraint, not because His reckless message finally caught up with Him. Jesus assured us that every time it seemed He was being forced against His will, He wasn't. He was choosing that. Embracing that moment, the culmination of God's redemptive plan for mankind. All of heaven waited with baited breath as the King became the Lamb and humanity was finally rescued.

Jesus desired with desire to offer His body, His blood, this bread, this cup.

"Do this in remembrance of Me." Here I got stuck. Do what? What do You mean by *do*? Is this a simple matter of observing the Lord's Supper once a quarter? Was Jesus emphasizing the Jewish custom of ritual, just with new symbolism? Let's mimic smart theologians and go Greek. "Do" is from *poieo*, which means, um, "do." So, okay. That trick wasn't helpful.

The important "do" aspect is how Jesus used the present tense, indicating continuous action, as opposed to the aorist imperative (forgive annoying terminology reserved for seminary students anxious to term-drop), implying a single action. It's the difference between "*Make* your bed," and "*Make* good choices." Once versus perpetual. When Jesus said of the wine in Luke 22:17, "Take this and divide it among you," that was a onetime command. But when He said, "Do this in remembrance of Me," it required continuous action.

Not only does Jesus' statement require a constant response, but *remembrance* is from *anamnesis*, meaning "to make real." Communion is more than a memory, more than a reverent moment when we recall Jesus' heroic sacrifice. Remembrance means honoring Jesus' mercy mission with tangible, physical action since it was a tangible, physical sacrifice. In other words, "*Constantly make this real.*"

The Lord Jesus, on the night he was betrayed, took bread, and when he had given thanks, he broke it and said, "This is my body, which is for you; do this in remembrance of me." (1 Corinthians 11:23-24)

Now you are the body of Christ. (1 Corinthians 12:27)

Not only was Communion a symbolic ritual, it was a new prototype of discipleship. "Continuously make My sacrifice real by doing *this very thing*." Become broken and poured out for hopeless people. Become a living offering, denying yourself for the salvation and restoration of humanity. Obedience to Jesus' command is more than looking backward; it's a present and continuous replication of His sacrifice. We don't simply remember the meal; we become the meal.

Doesn't this concept of being broken for others ring true? It's a spiritual dynamic that bears out physically. Why is it so exhausting to uphold someone's heavy, inconvenient burden? Why are we spent from shouldering someone's grief or being an armor bearer? Why is it that lifting someone out of his or her rubble leaves us breathless? Because we are the body of Christ, broken and poured out, just as He was.

Mercy has a cost: someone must be broken for someone else to be fed. The sermon that changed your life? That messenger was poured out so you could hear it. The friends who stood in the gap during your crisis? They embraced some sacrifice of brokenness for your healing. Anytime you say, "That fed me, that nourished me," someone was the broken bread for your fulfillment.

Carrying on the life of Christ is somehow integrated with

the concept of death. There is a death/life rhythm that sustains creation. Much like a seed is destroyed to produce a living tree or a vegetable is plucked from its vine to nourish a living body, self-sacrifice is hardwired into the mission of a believer. Brian McLaren wrote in *The Secret Message of Jesus*,

> What if our only hope lies in this impossible paradox, the only way the *kingdom of God* can be strong in a truly liberating way is through a scandalous, noncoercive kind of weakness; the only way it can be powerful is through astonishing vulnerability; the only way it can live is by dying?[5]

That helps me better understand Paul's teaching to the Corinthian church:

> We always carry around in our body the death of Jesus, so that the life of Jesus may also be revealed in our body. For we who are alive are always being given over to death for Jesus' sake, so that his life may be revealed in our mortal body. So then, death is at work in us, but life is at work in you. (2 Corinthians 4:10-12)

Death in me = life in you. Broken so someone else is fed. "Feed My lambs."

TOUGH CROWD

I was connecting the dots, and now I had a situation on my hands. I began wrestling with what this sort of life looked like. I'd already gotten the "Feed My sheep" memo. God was ruining me for justice, and in some way, this would require a willing brokenness. Not the kind that is little more than an inconvenience, a fissure in my wholeness. If I were to do this in remembrance of Jesus, with the same motive and manner, I would have to address some hard questions.

Starting with: Who was Jesus broken and poured out for? Luke told us Jesus said "for you" (Luke 22:19), Matthew and Mark report Him saying "for many" (Matthew 26:28; Mark 14:24), and Matthew added "for the forgiveness of sins."

(John skipped the Passover retelling and instead recorded Jesus washing the disciples' feet, for which we owe him eternal gratitude.) Perhaps the most astounding thing about Jesus' death on the cross is who He died for.

Sure, He did say "for you" to His disciples. Granted, they were a mixed blessing and pretty much didn't get Jesus until He was gone, but they loved Him. They followed Him. They embraced some element of self-denial to be Jesus' protégés. They were like big dumb animals who meant well and would fortunately one day transform from boys to men. These are people I like to think of Jesus dying for. You know, the ones who wrote a bunch of the Bible later. Died for their faith and such.

These are the types I want to be broken for too. If I'm picking whom I sacrifice for, I'm thinking future martyrs, gospel writers, and world changers. I love to pour into believers who take Jesus seriously. Eager learners who pester me with burning questions about Scripture that keep them up at night. These are my people. Love. You. In fact, this *was* who I served. I ministered to the convinced who preferred a table in the upper room.

(And can't we agree there is something compelling about extremists? It is easier to temper passion with discernment than apathy with zeal. I'd prefer a fanatical loose cannon over a bored yes-man any day. There are exceptions: My friend Trina encountered a mom whose daughter came to play with her then–fifth grader. Somewhere between this mom manually checking all Trina's smoke alarms, administering an interrogation *and* inspection for household guns, and installing her twelve-year-old's *car seat* in Trina's minivan, Trina realized she'd seen the face of crazy. This girl had a zero percent chance of injury but a good-to-excellent chance of becoming a serial killer. Sometimes, too much is too much.)

So anyway, this convinced demographic worked for me, or at least it was familiar. The pesky part came when the question burrowed deeper, since Judas was also part of the "for you" group Jesus referred to. Now we had a problem because this didn't square. Remember, I'm filtering this through the grid of social action and physical need, and I realized who Judas represented: those who would turn on me despite what I sacrificed or why.

If I didn't grasp that then, I'm getting it now. It's something like the homeless man I served a burger to in 105-degree heat who told me, "I hope this satisfies your white guilt for the day." And the addict we supported in every conceivable way who went back to heroin and never called again. And the young man we helped out of the shelter who spent the money we gave him on new piercings and a Bluetooth. And the believers who thought we were crazy.

This facet of broken and poured out for you? Not what I envisioned. A romanticized notion of social compassion gets trashed once you actually turn your bias to the bottom. It is far more nuanced than the pamphlets let on. This is where sometimes instead of a "thank you," you get a "!%&# you." Deep disappointment exists here. Betrayal resides here.

Rip-your-eyes-out frustration lives here. Inflated White Savior Complex lives (and must die) here. Hooray! Anyone still want to join me?

This was one reason I was detached from the margins, citing irresponsibility and recklessness and thanklessness. *They'll spend it on booze. Government is corrupt and shouldn't be helped. Get off your lazy butt and get a job, and then we'll talk.* I was shockingly ignorant about the cycles of poverty and addiction. (During a recent presidential election, a girl I know posted online, "Hey, poor people! Here's some advice: Have the good common sense not to get sucked into poverty!" and I almost shoved my head through a plate-glass window.) Nor did I even remotely understand the difference between empowering and enabling. So much of our initial "help" was so not helpful. Ignorant intervention is absolutely a contributing factor to cycles of oppression.

This is what God taught me through Judas at Jesus' table, eating the broken bread that was His body: We don't get to opt out of living on mission because we might not be appreciated. We're not allowed to neglect the oppressed because we have reservations about their discernment. We cannot deny love because it might be despised or misunderstood. We can't withhold social relief because we're not convinced it will be perfectly managed. We can't project our advantaged perspective onto struggling people and expect results available only to the privileged. Must we be wise? Absolutely. But doing nothing is a blatant sin of omission. Turning a blind eye to the bottom on the grounds of "unworthiness" is the antithesis to Jesus' entire mission. How dare we? Most of us know nothing, *nothing* of the struggles of the poor. We erroneously think ourselves superior, and it is a wonder God would use us at all to minister to His beloved.

Jesus came to the foulest, filthiest place possible (earth), a place full of ungrateful, self-destructive people who would betray Him far more than they'd love Him (a whole planet of Judases). He broke His body for rich people who would curse Him the second their prosperity was endangered. He poured His blood out for those who would take His Word and use it as a bludgeoning tool. He became the offering for people who would slander His name with ferocity, yet His grace was theirs for the asking until they drew their last breaths, even if all they could offer Him was a lifetime of hatred and one moment of repentance.

When Jesus' followers asked what to do about the weeds in the harvest field, He said to treat them the same as the wheat, "because while you are pulling the weeds, you may uproot the wheat with them" (Matthew 13:29). There was one Judas, but eleven disciples who were forever transformed by Jesus' broken body. The risk of encountering a few weeds is not sufficient reason to avoid the whole field of human suffering, because I assure you, identifying with the wheat but not the weeds is a gross overestimation of our own station. The correct character to identify with here is the weed shown mercy, not the Savior capable of discerning the human heart. Our holy Savior advised us well:

humans must treat the wheat and weeds the same. We are only qualified to administer mercy, not judgment, because we will pull up many a beautiful stalk of wheat, imagining him a weed.

Brandon's Take

"God, *if* You're really in this, show me, too."

I knew it was a dangerous prayer. But I meant it. While Jen was on the ride of her life, I began mine. It felt right and dangerous. I opened my mind to consider not what I was doing but why I was doing it. I began to evaluate my priorities and how I measured success. I listed how many things I did for others where I benefited nothing; the list was terribly small. It was glaringly obvious that my life and ministry were far more about me than about God and others.

I began to pray as never before. And I studied the Bible looking for one answer: "Lord, do You really want me to change the way I care for, minister to, and think about others, especially the least of these?"

Then they came: multiple encounters where Jesus showed up more powerfully than I've ever experienced. During that season, it was mostly through the homeless community, the people who could offer me nothing for my efforts. Or so I thought. Throughout the spring, I had several divine encounters that were such obvious "yes, I'm in this" confirmations that they still give me chills. Here's one of them:

It was my day off. I'd been pressing heavily into God, asking Him to show me the areas in my life that needed change. After listening to a podcast centered on creating margins in our lives for God to move, I decided to test the waters and just be available to be a blessing that day, to whomever.

Leaving the house, I had the strong impression that I would serve a homeless man that day. After telling Jen that revelation and hearing her response—"Good luck with that"—I jumped in my truck and asked God, "There are so many homeless in Austin. How will I know which one? Will he be on a specific street corner? Will it be obvious?"

God quickly responded in my spirit: "You'll know."

I drove to a used-car lot to visit with an acquaintance who worked there. He was going through some tough times, so I went to lend an ear. After about an hour, I noticed him staring over my left shoulder with a perplexed look on his face. I turned to see what had caught his attention, and I was floored.

Standing ten feet behind me was a deaf homeless man. He was dirty from head to toe, had an old backpack thrown over his shoulder, was staring me right in the eyes, and was motioning with his right hand, pointing to a brand-new picture of Jesus in his left hand.

I got chills over every inch of my entire body. I knew that God was speaking to me.

I spent the day with the man. I met his wife (who had cancer), shared a meal with them, and took them grocery shopping. I helped with some immediate needs at the day-rate motel they were about to get kicked out of. It was one of the most fulfilling days I'd had in years.

The rest of the story came later when I went to my office. Driving there, I reflected on the day and realized how selfishly concerned I was about the money I was out. Because we'd recently remodeled our kitchen, I'd just lectured Jen (I lecture—sorry, Jen) to stop spending money until payday. I added up how much it had cost me that day to serve a complete stranger. It totaled $195.

Still thinking about the money, I entered my office and saw an envelope with my name on it. Inside was an unexpected check written out to me. It was a reimbursement I had forgotten about and had no idea was coming. The check was for $195.

God was speaking loudly. He wasn't saying, "Bless others and I'll give you money"; He was saying, "The provision was not from you; it was from Me. What you have is not yours. You have a lot to learn. The first is this: you can trust Me when I call."

BECOMING
A LOWLIFE

The next movement in the story reminds me of the day I received my first book in the mail. I had the entire book memorized (editing involves approximately seven thousand rounds of rereading your own material—super fun!), I'd received the cover design in a JPEG file, I'd read the back-cover copy, I'd signed off on the color scheme. I'd seen the whole book in pieces. But nothing prepares you for lifting your first book out of a box and seeing—against all odds and reason—a real finished product with your name on it.

My daughter, Sydney, six at the time, happened to be there when UPS delivered the package. It came a week earlier than expected, so I was completely unprepared for book euphoria, and she was the only spectator in the Jen Receiving Her First Book in the Mail show. This was the culmination of so much work, the realization of a dream seeded in my heart.

I'd envisioned a scene reminiscent of the one in *Back to the Future* when made-over George McFly opened his first novel and quipped, "You see, Marty, if you put your mind to it, you can accomplish anything," while everyone looked on adoringly and Biff waxed their cars.[1] I grabbed Sydney's hand and forced her to witness the opening of the box. And there it was. They had really published it. I covered my mouth and worked up some melodramatic tears to punctuate the scene . . . and then Sydney the Buzzkill looked at me and asked, "What's for dinner?"

She had clearly missed the gravity of the occasion and ruined my McFly moment. Six-year-olds are unparalleled narcissists. Except for maybe the disciples, because not three seconds after this monumental Last Supper teaching by Jesus, "a dispute also arose among them as to which of them was considered to be greatest" (Luke 22:24). Unbelievable. If their insensitivity weren't so tragic, it would almost be funny.

Now, if I were Jesus (horror), I would've gone all Russell Crowe on everyone. The lecture the disciples received as I restated the whole "This is My body, stupids" lesson would have been unprecedented. If they missed the point the first go-round, they would certainly have gotten it twelve hours later after I was done with them. When faced with their obvious ignorance, I would have simply repeated what I'd already said but with anger and probably sarcasm.

But Jesus took a better approach. He chose to make the same point with a fresh illustration. If the "what" was to become broken and poured out for the restoration of hopeless humanity, then Jesus now explained the "how." Consequently, this part confirmed my suspicion that brokenness was going to hurt.

He segued by saying, "The kings of the Gentiles lord it over them; and those who exercise authority over them call themselves Benefactors" (Luke 22:25). That was familiar to the men: "Benefactor" was a title assumed by rulers in Egypt, Syria, and Rome as a display of honor, though it had no bearing on actual service rendered to the people. Rather, these rulers were consumed with promotion and accumulation. The people they led were a means to their own end, a bargaining chip for more power and prestige.

As much as culture has changed, it has in other ways remained exactly the same. In his book *Simplicity*, Richard Rohr wrote,

> Jesus' harshest words are aimed at hypocrites, and the second harshest at the people who are primarily concerned with possessions. He says that power, prestige, and possessions are the three things that prevent us from recognizing and receiving the reign of God. . . . The only ones who can accept the proclamation of the reign are those who have nothing to protect, not their own self-image or their reputation, their possessions, their theology, their

principles, or their certitudes. And these are called "the poor," *anawim* in Hebrew.[2]

Blessed are the poor, for theirs is the kingdom of God (Luke 6:20).

I'm learning what it means to descend, which is so revolutionary it often leaves me gasping. I have been trying to ascend my entire life. Up, up, next level, a notch higher, the top is better, top of the food chain, all for God's work and glory, of course. The pursuit of ascension is crippling and has stunted my faith more than any other evil I've battled. It has saddled me with so much to defend, and it doesn't deliver. I need more and more of what doesn't work. I'm insatiable, and ironically, the more I accumulate, the less I enjoy any of it. Instead of satisfaction, it produces toxic fear in me; I'm always one slip away from losing it all.

Consequently, my love for others is tainted because they unwittingly become articles for consumption. How is this person making me feel better? How is she making me stronger? How is he contributing to my agenda? What can this group do for me? I am an addict, addicted to the ascent and thus positioning myself above people who can propel my upward momentum and below those who are also longing for a higher rank and might pull me up with them. It feels desperate and frantic, and I'm so done being enslaved to the elusive top rung.

When Jesus told us to "take the lowest place" (Luke 14:10), it was more than a strategy for social justice. It was even more than wooing us to the bottom for communion, since that is where He is always found. The path of descent becomes our own liberation. We are freed from the exhausting stance of defense. We are no longer compelled to be right and are thus relieved from the burden of maintaining some reputation. We are released from the idols of greed, control, and status. The pressure to protect the house of cards is alleviated when we take the lowest place.

The ascent is so ingrained in my thought patterns that it has been physically painful to experience reformation at the bottom. The compulsion to defend myself against misrepresentation nearly put me in the grave recently. I was tormented with chaotic inner dialogues, and there were days I was so plagued with protecting my rung that I couldn't get out of bed. With every step lower, the stripping-away process was more excruciating. I had no idea how tightly I clung to reputation and approval or how selfishly I behaved to maintain it. Getting to the top requires someone else to be on the bottom; being right means someone else must be wrong. It is the nature of the beast.

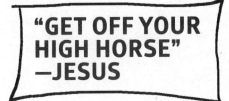

"GET OFF YOUR HIGH HORSE" —JESUS

"But you are not to be like that," said Jesus (Luke 22:26). When believers play by the rules of power, we become Benefactors, using those we are charged to serve and cutting off those who no longer advance our agenda. Jesus' point was clear: *Don't get sucked into the game.* Be countercultural. Be the opposite of great. If that means others are ahead of you, so what? If people criticize your method or motive, what difference does it make?

If you're removed from the map of recognition? Good. About time.

I hate the top. I hate who I have to be to live there. I hate the biblical two-step I have to perform to justify top-dwelling.

I hate the posturing up there. I can't stand the fear of heights, since falling is a constant danger. I can't bear how far it is from the Spirit who said He was "close to the brokenhearted" (Psalm 34:18) and that "the highborn are but a lie" (Psalm 62:9). I detest the fear that haunts every decision. It's a ridiculous game where everyone is either scratching your back or stabbing you in the back, depending on whether your rung is above or below theirs. The self-congratulatory blustering up there is abhorrent.

I'm so over it.

Okay, maybe it would be more true to say I so *want* to be over it. I'm trying to be over it. I see the ascent for what it is, and I'm tired just looking at it. When I'm not climbing it, of course.

I found the descent to be terribly painful, and confronting my own selfishness was excruciating. I remember days when I wanted to crawl out of my skin, so uncomfortable was the deconstruction. I often thought, *I'll never be happy again. The screaming voices in my head will never be silent.* I had Jesus tugging me downward and "self" hanging on to my rung with white knuckles. Every new conviction was like a dagger. My default responses were invalid, and all I had left was humility. Which has never been my strong suit. In order for God's kingdom to come, my kingdom had to go.

Silver lining: once you hit bottom and recover somewhat from the descent, it is shockingly peaceful down there. It's much quieter. The chaos of ego and pride recedes. It's, well, kind of still and beautiful. I find myself exhaling and thinking less about the race going on up higher. Releasing the compulsion to be right, to be respected, to be understood, to be winning—if not natural, it's certainly a relief.

It's as if Jesus knew that the secret of life awaits us at the bottom. Oh wait, that is *exactly* what He said, all the time, in every possible way, through parable and story, by example and modeling, directly and indirectly, corporately and privately. Shane Claiborne wrote,

> Jesus did not seek out the rich and powerful in order to trickle down his kingdom. Rather, he joined those at the bottom, the outcasts and undesirables, and everyone was attracted to his love for people on the margins. . . . Then he invited everyone into a journey of downward mobility to become the least.[1]

If the kingdom of God belongs to the poor, the bottom dwellers, then rich American Christians are going to have the hardest time finding it. The whole filthy engine is designed to benefit the top, and that is our zip code. Perhaps this is why the church is gaining ground in impoverished and oppressed regions but declining in the United States and affluent continents like Europe and Australia. The needy world isn't interested in God because He might secure their promotion or deliver an offer on their house in a wilting market. By the millions, they are running to the cross because the love of a redeeming Savior is too intoxicating to resist. Jesus is their hope and inheritance, and they glory in Him despite crushing poverty, political upheaval, and endless instability. They already live at the bottom, in Jesus' zip code.

They are so much closer to the secret of life than we are. I worry sometimes that it is impossible for me to truly identify with Christ since I am at the top of the global food chain: white, American, educated, affluent, healthy, Texan (wink). I'm at the apex on the pyramid scheme, already enjoying every benefit and advantage everyone else is laboring for. The rest of the world struggles with hunger and sickness, but we have to conquer the diseases of greed and ego, which are notoriously harder to cure. When Jesus said, "It is easier for a camel to go through the eye of a needle than for someone who is rich to enter the kingdom of God" (Matthew 19:24), I now understand that's me. And you. The higher we are, the harder it is to adopt the heart of Christ. I suppose that's why Americans are the richest people on the planet but plagued with depression, suicide, and loneliness. We're furthest from the freedom that exists only at the bottom, and money can't buy that liberation.

GREAT

"We cannot do great things, only small things with great love."
—MOTHER TERESA

What alternative to fighting our way up the ladder do we have? It's pretty simple and awful, I'm afraid. As nineteenth-century Danish philosopher Søren Kierkegaard wrote,

> Take any words in the New Testament and forget everything except pledging yourself to act accordingly. My God, you will say, if I do that my whole life will be ruined. How would I ever get on in the world?
>
> Herein lies the real place of Christian scholarship. Christian scholarship is the church's prodigious invention to defend itself against the Bible, to ensure that we can continue to be good Christians without

the Bible coming too close. Oh, priceless scholarship, what would we do without you? Dreadful it is to fall into the hands of the living God. Yes, it is even dreadful to be alone with the New Testament.[1]

Indeed.

When Jesus spoke, it was the "losers" who understood while the "winners" were stumped and called Him a lunatic. We almost have to be marginalized to become capable of hearing the gospel. On the margins, as Richard Rohr explained, Jesus' social implications are crystal clear:

> There we learn that we can't use Jesus to defend and maintain our position of power and wealth or to keep up for our own sake a positive self-image as polite and decent people. It could be that Jesus will lead us to a place where we ourselves don't even know whether we're holy, where all we know is that we have work to do, where we have to obey the word that we've heard in our heart.[2]

After exposing the Benefactors, Jesus elaborated on the posture of a true disciple: "The greatest among you should be like the youngest" (Luke 22:26).

I get why Jesus used *youngest* here. When my son Caleb was younger, he was a loyal disciple to his older siblings. Despite his worship of them, he was always in last place. He came in one day sobbing, "We were playing a game where we did a funny act in front of each other, and then we got scored. Gavin and Sydney were so funny and they gave each other eights and nines, because they thought they were so awesome, but when I did my act, they only gave me half a point, because *my act is so lame!*" I assure you, Caleb is not lame (ask anyone). He is, unknowingly, the funniest kid on the planet. But by *youngest*, I think Jesus meant becoming content with half a point instead of an eight or nine. "I chose you out of the world, therefore the world hates you" (John 15:19, NKJV). Get used to it.

> And the one who rules [should be] like the one who serves. For who is greater, the one who is at the table or the one who serves? (Luke 22:26-27)

This moment makes me laugh because I envision a pregnant pause while the disciples tried to figure out the right response. It was rarely the obvious answer with Jesus, so I can see them staring at His mouth, watching for a consonant to form to give them a clue. "It's the one who . . . is . . . at the . . . table or serving . . . with the food . . . and the guy . . ." Bless 'em.

> Is it not the one who is at the table? (Luke 22:27)

"Yes! That's it! The one at the table! I was thinking it was the one at the table! I knew it, but I thought He was tricking us again!" Make no mistake: culture has and always will tell us that the one being served is greater. The table dweller has arrived. He is our standard and goal. It's great to be him, no doubt about it.

But I am among you as one who serves. (Luke 22:27)

Jesus had already made a strong case for the descent: Become broken and poured out for others, constantly make this real, desire with desire to sacrifice, resist the power politics of the Benefactors. But in His closing statement, He called Himself a servant, making this worldview nearly impossible to spin or misconstrue.

Is this not why the gospel is such good news for the broken? Jesus redefined the nature of greatness, which has always rung hollow for the least and last. He took its connotation away from power and possessions and bestowed it on the humility of a servant. The more you defer? The more grateful you are to be broken and poured out? The more you choose servant over Benefactor?

The greater you are.

So be it in my life, and so be it in the church. May intentional servanthood be the basis of all mission, all benevolence, all evangelism, all sacrifice. I dream of a church that is once again called great, even by our skeptics, because our works of mercy cannot be denied. I want no part in a movement that is deemed great because we've adopted some exceptional qualities admired by the top.

I don't want to be known for a great band.

I don't want to be admired for a great campus.

I don't want to be recognized for a great marketing campaign.

I don't want to be praised for great programming.

I don't want to be applauded for great theology and scholarship.

I want the church to be great because we fed hungry mommas and their babies. I'd like to be great because we battled poverty with not just our money but our hands and hearts. I desire the greatness that comes from seeking not only mercy but justice for those caught in a system with trapdoors. I hope to be part of a great movement of the Holy Spirit, who injects supernatural wind and fire into His mission. My version of great will come when others are scratching their heads and saying, "Wow, you live a really different life."

For it is the one who is least among you all who is the greatest. (Luke 9:48)

Heavy Influences—Phase Two

- *Simplicity* by Richard Rohr
- *Isn't She Beautiful?* Mars Hill church conference
- *Mother Teresa: In My Own Words* by Mother Teresa
- *The Kite Runner* by Khaled Hosseini
- *My Sister, My Brother* by Henri J. M. Nouwen
- *Rich Christians in an Age of Hunger* by Ronald J. Sider
- *Don't Waste Your Life* by John Piper

PHASE THREE:
GETTING OUT THERE

We see a church that cares passionately for the oppressed,
the abandoned, the helpless, and those in spiritual, relational,
emotional, and physical need. We believe it is the church's
responsibility to lead this movement both in our community
and throughout the world.

VALUE:
Serving others selflessly and sacrificially.

KEY SCRIPTURE:
Matthew 25

HERE PRETENDING
TO BE THERE

Some parents pray for their children's future spouses with an emphasis on certain qualities. Evidently, traits like godliness and humility are things to major on. This is cute and all, but in the family I grew up in, we engaged in a different sort of prayer. See, we are a loud and funny tribe, and joining us is not for the faint of heart (or the lame). Our spousal applicants *could* demonstrate godliness and all that, but what really separated them from inferior candidates was how they performed on our primary King Family Assessment: Are they funny?

My sister Cortney's selection, Zac, proved himself a contender as he demonstrated advanced skills in dry wit and banter. During Zac's trial period (read: he dated Cortney while we made judgments behind his back), he secured his position as top nominee when we saw his backyard.

It was vintage white trash, complete with half-broken chairs and Christmas lights. Next to the well-worn dog run—you guessed it: Rottweiler Alert—was a Man Grill that cost more than my car. (Zac is a competitive barbecuer, which certainly didn't hurt his running tally.) Strewn around the yard were massacred remains of the trash, plus fluffy bits of shredded cushions against which the rotty waged daily war. All this made an ideal backdrop for the crown jewel: an aboveground pool with a pesky filtration system that couldn't conquer the top layer of leaves and film. But the moment we knew that Zac would—nay, *should*—become ours is when we saw the hand-painted plywood sign staked into the ground:

"Zacapulco."

Not only did we snatch him off the open market and claim him for ourselves, we've also since adopted his inventive use of tropical irony for our yards:

Brandon and Jen Hatmaker + Puerto Vallarta =
  "Hat-o-Vallarta"
Larry and Jana King + Key Largo = "King Largo"
Drew King + Cabo San Lucas = "Cabo San Drewcas"
Lindsay King + Cancun = "Kingcun"

Our friends think our game is fun, and many named their own backyard paradises:

Andy and Anna Melvin + Cozumel = "Cozumelvin"
Tray and Jenny Pruet + Puerto Rico = "Pruet Rico"
Andrew and Trina Barlow + Nuevo Laredo = "Nuevo
     Barledo"

It's common lingo among our friends-and-family clan
("Come hang out on Hat-o-Vallarta!" "Party at Cozumelvin!").
Brandon and I even have a sign of individually carved letters
complete with palm trees, thanks to Tray of the Pruet Rico
tribe, who thought Hat-o-Vallarta deserved proper signage.

I guess the reason we have to post signs to remind us
where we are is because we're not really at our destination.
We're using the terminology and borrowing the symbolism;
we're making labels and showcasing our preferences. But at
the end of the day, we're *here* pretending to be *there*.

A frustrating trait about God is how He expects us to act on
conviction fairly quickly. Pretty much the second He convinces
us to move, to change, to shift, we're supposed to. Despite how
much we ponder it or talk about it, until we are obedient in
word and deed, we're just here pretending to be there.

As God shifted our story, we faced a quick progression:
He first captured our minds—convicting us of apathy and
opening our eyes to human suffering. Then He seized our
hearts—instilling desire for life and service at the bottom.
And quickly thereafter was the call to our hands: Get moving. Because, as James basically said, if all we do is talk theology and pat the forsaken on the head with a hearty "Best of
luck with that need!" what good is it? (See James 2:16.)

Mind → heart → hands. Lord, help us.

DON'T KNOW IF WE'RE COMING OR GOING

Mind → heart → hands.

In theory? Doable. In practice? Paralysis. In our church context, we had no idea what to do. We were familiar with an attractional model, which is somewhat successful if the target audience has a context for church. "Build it and they will come" works for those who want a building and feel like coming to it. The ministries, programs, volunteers, staff, nearly all human and financial resources serve the weekend attendees. This was the model I grew up in, and to be sure, I am thankful for the foundation in Christ (plus its cool church store to buy my very awesome Christian T-shirts with lovely slogans like "Get Right . . . or Get Left!" which, surprisingly, netted exactly zero converts).

In addition to regular church folks, we'd been given a new "they," and that included those in physical, emotional, and financial crisis. But if "they" had to come to "us" for a human touch, this left us in the lurch. What about the really broken people who can't or won't find their way to us? What about those too frozen in suffering to consider a nine-thirty or eleven o'clock service? And, also, what about the people who despise church and Christians and can't for the life of them figure out what is "good" about our good news? What about the spiritually hungry who keep leaving churches uninspired and unmoved? What if we need to go to them instead of hoping they'll come to us?

Which raises a question: Are they coming to us?

This never crossed my mind because in my church microcosm, they seemed to be coming. Well, they were coming and going, at least. I hadn't considered the church at large or peeked over my own fence at what was happening out there. (Ignorance? Is not bliss.) So when I did, I discovered this giant conversation weaving among millions of believers who were rethinking a church that wasn't attracting people like it used to. They were struggling with figures like:

- Only three out of ten twentysomethings attend church in a typical week, compared to four out of ten thirtysomethings, and five out of ten in their fifties and older.[1] While that sounds like a small decline, that three out of ten instead of a four or five out of ten represents millions of young adults rejecting the organized church. If the trend holds, the church is two or three generations away from mass cultural irrelevance.

- Six out of ten spiritually active teens left the church in their twenties.[2]
- 34 percent of the US adult population has not attended any type of church service or activity (other than weddings or funerals) during the past six months, about 73 million adults.
- Roughly 62 percent of all unchurched adults were formerly churched.[3] Let that sink in. Not only can we not draw new people, we can't keep the ones we have.
- Approximately half of all American churches did not add one new person through conversion growth last year.[4]
- More than 80 percent of the current growth registered by Protestant churches is biological or transfer growth, meaning new children are born into the church or believers are church hopping.[5] We're not adding to the kingdom; we're simply reshuffling the deck.
- In America, it takes the combined effort of eighty-five Christians working over an entire year to produce one convert.[6]
- In a nationwide survey, 94 percent of churches either were not growing or were losing ground in the communities they serve.[7]
- Thom Rainer and his research team predicted correctly that fifty thousand churches would close by 2010, roughly one in every eight.[8]

I know statistics can say anything, and wading through these left me grouchy and fuzzy. But no matter how you slice it, millions of Christians have left the organized church in the last twenty years, and we're not drawing the next generation. The trend is clearly downward, and at this pace, reimagining church in America is not just the task of mavericks; it will require the whole bride. This is happening. Stick your head in the ground like an ostrich if you wish, but perhaps it would be more helpful and courageous to admit we have a problem and begin dreaming up solutions.

The world is increasingly uninterested in our Christian story. Our current presentation is just not compelling. Most believers who represent it battle boredom and apathy; they are spiritually immature and demonstrate religiosity without transformation. We launch public shame grenades with abandon and claim to "love the sinner but hate the sin," which translates to "we are enormous pompous jerks." Our faith communities run the gamut from judgmental high church to feel-good talent shows, and people aren't buying anymore. Remarkably, most outsiders are not anti-church (our gospel isn't provocative enough to incite backlash anymore); they simply dismiss the church as irrelevant to their real lives since it seems mostly irrelevant to the people who go there.

"Christianity has lost its place as the center of American life," wrote Tom Clegg and Warren Bird in *Lost in America*. "Christians must learn how to live the gospel as a distinct people who no longer occupy the center of society. We must learn to build relational bridges that win a hearing."[9] Our

Christian rhetoric has become white noise, I'm afraid. It gets hopelessly stuck in our minds (read: mouths) and struggles to transition to our hearts and then hands.

Our only hope is to follow the example of Jesus and get back out there, winning people over with ridiculous love and a lifestyle that causes them to finally sit up and take notice. Listen, no church can ever do this for me—not one who once hired us, not one we started, not an invented one in our imaginations. This is my high calling: to live on mission as an adopted daughter of Jesus. If people around me aren't moved by my Christ or my church, then I must be doing a miserable job of representing them both.

In *The Tangible Kingdom*, Hugh Halter and Matt Smay wrote,

> Change must be about new [hello, word of the month], which to us means "fresh, bright, something that intuitively feels right, that causes us not only to dream but to move on our dreams." That kind of new is good if it compels us into a world of faith again where we can battle fear and despondency with action that makes a difference. That kind of new is okay, but it really isn't new. It's just been hidden, or covered, or we've been distracted from it. . . .
>
> This type of new is about a returning. Returning to something ancient, something tried, something true and trustworthy. Something that has rerouted the legacies of families, nations, kings, and peasants.

Something that has caused hundreds of thousands to give up security, reputation, and their lives. . . . What we need to dig up, recover, and find again is the life of the Kingdom and Jesus' community . . . the church. . . . It's not anti-church; it's pro-church. It's about the type of church that Jesus would go to, the type he died to give flight to.[10]

JUSTICE
FOR JESUS

I am being lured back to the way of Jesus. I am finding it so—sorry for this—spiritual. I'd kind of forgotten how compelling the Spirit is. He is the fresh wind everyone is looking for. He reminds me I am a member of a grand assembly that inspires and stirs and empowers. On bad days, when I secretly whisper, "Is this all there is?" the Spirit urges me to join Him at the bottom, where the best grassroots movements have always begun.

He is the *new* I was craving when I realized my heart was dry. Paul explained that "we serve in the new way of the Spirit" (Romans 7:6), and I deeply considered that for the first time. (My spouse ultimately made that verse his mantra and tattooed it all over his arm. We sell out in this family.) But how? How was I to serve in the new way of the Spirit? What did that mean? And if that service involved *me going* instead of *them coming*, I was leaving my safety zone, where I knew the rules and had collaborators, where I was a little popular and God was the soup du jour. I wasn't sure what to do. So I asked.

Cut to Matthew 25:31-46, a passage I had never in my life taken seriously. It begins with Jesus describing this final drama: "When the Son of Man comes in his glory, and all the angels with him, he will sit on his glorious throne. All the nations will be gathered before him" (verses 31-32). Having endured sermonizing on Judgment Day and the Four Horsemen of the Apocalypse my entire childhood, I took something of a sabbatical from the topic as an adult.

But after clearing the legalistic static, I saw two perspectives that now bring me comfort instead of turn-or-burn fear. The first is the basic foreknowledge that Jesus will get His just due. The humility of Christ has always given me problems. The description of His physical humiliation and the outright contempt He suffered silently—these accounts give me severe spiritual anxiety. The dishonor heaped on God incarnate has always assaulted my sense of justice, leaving me raw and unsettled. The silent, will-not-defend-myself posture Jesus maintained fries a circuit in my brain. I have always needed closure on the sins against Him. Justice for Jesus, if you will.

"He will sit on his throne in heavenly glory" does the

trick nicely. I feel such relief when I read about Jesus' eternal glory. All is set right in my world; I don't have to accept the injustice He accepted. One day all His haters and critics and doubters and mockers will be unable to hate and criticize and doubt and mock because Jesus will come in full glory, the glory that belongs to Him alone, the glory He earned and deserves. Justice will be suspended no longer, and the King will get the worship He is owed. I realize Jesus reigned on the cross in humiliation, but I'm ready for Him to reign on the throne in glory. That is where my Jesus belongs. Until then, He waits patiently at the right hand of God, delaying His fame for the sake of one more believer, two more, three more . . .

His sacrifice for us continues.

Which brings me to my second thought. Thus far, the worst school discipline we've faced involved my sixth grader making sarcastic comments at inappropriate moments. (Do not say a word, reader.) There are little snafus, easily handled between me and the teacher, and my children go to the office only when pretending they're sick. (My kindergartener calling from the nurse's office: "My elbow hurts so bad, Mom. It's broken. And it itches.")

That said, we are on the front edge of high school, where things could get dicey. I fully expect my kids to be perfect, never mouth off, always turn in their AP work, and salvage their teachers' hope for the next generation. I daresay awards will be created to honor their impeccable behavior, given the extremely compliant DNA they were blessed with from model parents. However, should the bad kids negatively influence my good kids toward shenanigans (I'm planning to play that card), I have an ace up my sleeve, a little weapon I intend to use liberally and without reservation.

My mom is the high school principal.

I'm not saying she should give them preferential treatment and strategically place them with the best teachers (that is exactly what I'm saying), but there is comfort in knowing that if something goes wrong, if something heads south, if my kids end up facing the music, Principal King is also known as Grana. They will find mercy because they are her babies, and blood runs thick.

Having Jesus as Judge, like we see in Matthew 25, is something akin to having your Grana double as your principal. No one loves me more than Jesus. No one is more on my side. No one is more obsessed with His sons and daughters. No one else laid down His life to defend me. It's walking into court and finding out your best friend is hearing the case. If Jesus as Judge used to scare me, now it comforts me because "there is now no condemnation for those who are in Christ Jesus" (Romans 8:1). The Judge also goes by the name Friend. His justice is constructed on mercy, and I'll never stand before a Judge more determined to bring about my liberation.

A WORD ABOUT FARM ANIMALS

Jesus did paint a picture of a trial of sorts, and the issue at hand is pretty simple. There aren't a lot of gray areas. In fact, it's pretty cut-and-dried. He had a knack for taking something we overcomplicate and boiling it down to two options (two roads, two masters, two commandments, two sons, two houses):

> He will separate the people one from another as a shepherd separates the sheep from the goats. He will put the sheep on his right and the goats on his left.
>
> Then the King will say to those on his right, "Come, you who are blessed by my Father; take your

inheritance, the kingdom prepared for you since the creation of the world. For I was hungry and you gave me something to eat, I was thirsty and you gave me something to drink, I was a stranger and you invited me in, I needed clothes and you clothed me, I was sick and you looked after me, I was in prison and you came to visit me."

Then the righteous will answer him, "Lord, when did we see you hungry and feed you, or thirsty and give you something to drink? When did we see you a stranger and invite you in, or needing clothes and clothe you? When did we see you sick or in prison and go to visit you?"

The King will reply, "Truly I tell you, whatever you did for one of the least of these brothers and sisters of mine, you did for me." (Matthew 25:32-40)

Jesus was in the midst of teaching the disciples kingdom priorities. This was His final week; He knew it—they didn't. Much like a terminally ill patient speaks the most important words when death is near, Jesus now taught with urgency and priority. They had pressed Him for clarification on the end of the age, so Jesus explained a series of parables to help them wrap their minds around it.

Be like the wise, watchful servant, not the wicked, abusive one. Emulate the five wise virgins, not the foolish, sleepy ones. (Got that, guys?) Act like the servant with five invested talents, not the scaredy servant with one buried talent. And as Jesus built His case and the disciples began to gauge what counted and what wouldn't, He hit them with the grand finale: It will matter only if you're a sheep or a goat. The blessed and the lost will be separated based on one principle: the care of the oppressed. The end.

Perhaps the finest communicator to ever grace this planet, Jesus will play the role not only of Judge but King—and this passage in Matthew 25 is, in fact, the only instance when He gave Himself that title. He drew Himself up to full stature— all the power, all the position, all the authority He would willingly defer later that week. He was King supreme, and He alone would be sifting the wheat from the chaff. And in that paradoxical way of His, Jesus threw all His weight behind those at the very bottom of the pile. Last will be first. Blessed are the poor. Proud will be leveled.

His highest rank on behalf of the lowest class.

LAST BUT
NOT LEAST

Hungry. Thirsty. Lonely. Naked. Sick. Imprisoned. The messy reality of suffering is mentioned not once, not twice, but four times throughout this short parable. It's worth repeating, because although we've heard these words so often that they seem ordinary, they are actually some of the most revolutionary claims ever made. Immediately before the narrative of Jesus' passion and death, He presented the scene of the Last Judgment as a strategic metaphor wherein the least is identified with the Lord of history.

This parable is an indictment on humanity's violent resistance to God's revelation of the dignity of every human life. In the last century alone, millions have been killed in the

Middle East for the sake of homeland and nation. Six million Jews were systematically murdered during the horror of the Holocaust. Eleven million Hindus and Muslims were slaughtered at the dawn of Indian independence. Twenty million were massacred in the purging of Communist China. Rwanda, Serbia, Darfur all sank under the tidal wave of genocide. Men, women, and children of every color, tribe, race, and creed were bound, traded, and killed upon birth, such was their disvalue.

Away from the fields of war, unborn babies are destroyed in their mothers' wombs under the umbrella of preference. Seniors are cast aside in their twilight years, a burden on our ambitions. Our teens learn to kill with their words, repeating patterns they've learned from Hollywood and home. Our veterans sleep under bridges, forever damaged by trauma and neglect. The cycles of poverty churn out unparented children who act out with violence and confusion.

To such a bleak history, the King cries, "As often as you have done this to the least of these brothers and sisters of Mine, you have done it to Me." In the scope of human bedlam, we have maimed the body of Christ. The starving, the unwanted old and unborn, the criminal, those of wrong color, ideology, sex, nation, class—whatever category renders a person *least* in our minds—bear the face of Jesus.

It's so maddening and overwhelming that Christians pretend not to hear it. Or some spiritual two-stepping is involved to get out of it. A couple of interpretations exist wherein this scenario is simply a slice of what to expect during the Great Tribulation after you and I are safely raptured. Conveniently, this means we don't have to worry our little heads with the whole sheep-or-goat dilemma. So if you adhere to that dispensational interpretation, feel free to skip the next few paragraphs until I'm done ranting.

Of course, there is also the explanation posed by many scholars that these brothers and sisters of Jesus refer mainly to suffering believers and perhaps secondarily to all humanity, if at all. This reading is largely based on the habit Jesus made of calling believers "brothers" in the gospel of Matthew. If this is your position, let me say that if you want to start with the poor, sick, hungry, imprisoned believers of the world, then you'll have plenty to do, so go right ahead. Indeed, we have millions of impoverished brothers and sisters in Christ both at home and abroad, so that will certainly keep you busy. It is both a noble and necessary task.

As for me, I'm going to gamble on the fact that Jesus didn't have much patience with believers who attempted to limit the scope of "who my neighbor is" to the fewest possible people (see Luke 10:25-37). Jesus always colored outside of the lines here, extending grace and healing to those well beyond His people group. He often healed people first; they believed second. If I'm wrong, the worst thing that could happen is that some desperate people are cared for, and I'm guessing Jesus will look the other way. He seems to favor unmerited grace. To me, this is a wheat-and-weeds issue, and since that's not my call to make, I'll just err on the side of mercy and let Jesus sort it out at the harvest.

Jesus' identification with the least is the cornerstone of this parable. He tells of the day when the righteous will stand before Him, surprised at the credit they're receiving for caring. A popular interpretation exists wherein people who didn't know Jesus and certainly were not motivated by His kingdom will be welcomed as righteous simply for their attention to the least.

While my soft side loves that concept, I don't buy it. Many will stand before Jesus one day, clutching good works in their hands, but they will leave His presence because they never loved Him. If we've learned anything from the rebellious nation of Israel, the Pharisees and Sadducees, and the meager offerings of the poor in Scripture, it is this: God is supremely concerned with our motives, and our works count only when they match our intentions. There is no back door into salvation, rerouted around the sacrifice of Christ. Otherwise, the whole earth could gain heaven by good works, and His day on the cross would be pointless.

Jesus was describing the moment when His followers, His beloved sons and daughters, will stand before Him.

Of course we loved the poor, Jesus. You told us to. Of course we opened our homes and invited the lonely in. That was clear in the Word. Of course we clothed naked children and fed starving people. They are human beings made in Your image. We took care of the least in obedience to You, Jesus, but we never had the privilege of actually serving You.

We did all that *for* You.

But Jesus will say, no, you did that *unto* Me.

That's the shocker. It's not surprising that He is pleased when we adopt His bias toward the bottom. It's startling that He is actually served. We clearly don't comprehend how personally Jesus takes it when we love suffering people. He is so utterly identified with the afflicted that there is nothing more obedient, more pleasing, more central than serving Him in the marginalized. I wrote one time about being jealous of the disciples, how they knew the lines in Jesus' hands and the sound of His voice. They were chosen to experience Jesus in the flesh, a distinction they had no concept of until He was gone.

Yet a similar honor awaits us all. We have the privilege of serving Jesus Himself every time we feed a hungry belly, each moment we give dignity to someone who has none left, when we acknowledge the value of a convict because he is a human being, when we share our extreme excess with those who have nothing, when we love the forsaken and remember the forgotten. Jesus is there.

It's a spiritual mystery that leaves us scratching our heads as the righteous did in this story, yet a wisp of recognition rises up as I read Jesus' words. I've met Jesus at the bottom far more than I ever communed with Him at the top. Shane Claiborne described his experience at the Home for the Destitute and Dying when working with Mother Teresa in Calcutta:

As I looked into the eyes of the dying, I felt like I was meeting God. It was as if I were entering the

Holy of Holies in the temple—sacred, mystical.
I felt like I should take off my shoes. I knew what
Dorothy Day meant when she said, "The true atheist
is the one who denies God's image in the 'least of
these.'" The reality that God's Spirit dwells in each
of us began to sink in.[1]

It's not something I would have identified with earlier, but
since our life interruption, it is bizarre how many Scriptures
are becoming true to me in a new way. It's a different kind of
true—far removed from my head but lodged deeply somewhere in my gut, in my experience.

POOR PEOPLE

As I mentioned earlier, the next movement in our story was the call to get out there. Certainly, God had my attention.

And I was busy filling my mind and heart with all this, but as Franciscan priest Richard Rohr observed, "We cannot think our way into a new kind of living. We must live our way into a new kind of thinking."[1] (His book *Simplicity* is so brilliant and profound that I find myself wanting to plagiarize the entire thing.)

The Hatmaker tribe embarked on a stumbling, awkward journey downward. When I read about Shane Claiborne's experience in the Calcutta slums, Jeffrey Sachs' pilgrimage into the poorest African villages, and John Hayes' hospice work in Cambodia, I kind of want to laugh out loud and/ or cry at my own ridiculous foray into the world of poverty. You have to know that I hold none of this in high regard or think we're revolutionaries. I'm in the PTA, for Pete's sake. It's beyond humbling—it's embarrassing to admit that the saints have quietly done this work for centuries, and continue to do it today, with little or no recognition, while I lived my prosperous life, apathetic. I am simply scrambling behind, trying to catch up. I am more aware of my own poverty and smallness than ever, so don't imagine for a moment that this is a source of reverse spiritual pride.

On the contrary, my perspective of Jesus in the least has exposed my own apathy and ignorance and selfishness and ego so visibly that sometimes I wish I could go back. Then I could go to the optometrist without crying in the parking lot for fifteen minutes because I can afford the extravagant gift of good eyesight. It was less heart-wrenching to tuck my kids into bed without envisioning the millions of children who will sleep on dirt with no mother to attend to their needs that night. It was nice not to wrestle with sharing my excess, since I've tangled my life up with possessions and responsibilities already. I enjoyed not feeling raw all the time. I liked imagining I was something rather than realizing I am nothing. I can't unknow what I know, and I can't unsee what I've seen; it leaves me aching.

But every new season begins somewhere small, and thus we turned our eyes to the poor. This involved lots of time downtown feeding the hungry, picking up men with no legs (ask my kids about this) and taking them and others like them to dinner, transforming Valentine's Day into a family excursion to the darkest underbelly of Austin—stuff like that. We changed the way we celebrated holidays, attempting to filter them through the gospel instead of culture. We latched onto the informed and active, soaking up their knowledge and experience as sponges. We painfully overhauled our personal budget, freeing up some excess to share. We began chipping away at the walls we'd constructed between "us" and "them" and discovered common ground instead.

To say we were awkward and weird would be a kind understatement. Because my experience with poor people was limited, I placed the emphasis on poor but misunderstood the essential part: people. Which is the polar opposite perspective. When they were "poor" to me, then I was the benevolent, hyperfriendly white girl who had a hard time entering into a real conversation. The emphasis was on what I was offering: food, gloves, water, a bus pass. What I saw in them was *need*, so that is what I addressed. You require something; I'm here to deliver it with my White Savior Complex solidly in hand.

This is an okay place to start, but here is where that "Jesus did it for me" thing came in. I started noticing not so much their need but their humanity. I realized these were daddies and sisters and lost sons and daughters. They had stories and dreams. Their wallets were full of pictures, and their histories were full of heartache. They were funny and wildly talented. (Johnny the Bucket Drummer played at our new church once; he brought down the house.)

I am no Savior; I am just a sister.

We looked each other in the eyes, and we were the same—fragile humans who are patterned after Jesus, which makes us all beautiful. We're all poor; I just have more stuff. My affection for them became my offering, far more important than the food or clean socks I brought. A hot meal can't hold a candle to a real friend. Jesus ignited a love for people that burned white hot, a growing inferno out of the tiny spark He'd started earlier.

So as I was beginning to identify with the least—and Jesus already said He was the least—I was perhaps starting to commune with Christ in earnest for the first time in my life. It was a party at the bottom. Sorry I was so late. I got lost.

COLD WEATHER, CRAZY-LOOKING MESSENGER, AND RESURRECTION SUNDAY

Somewhere in the spring of 2007, Brandon and I looked at each other and said, "I wonder what all this means for us." We were experiencing some tension between our homeless street corners and our current post. Nothing as unfair as a good/bad or right/wrong conclusion—just terribly different. We were sort of living two separate lives, wondering how all this was going to reconcile.

Initially, it made perfect sense to stay put because Brandon was the pastor over spiritual development. We assumed God was instilling a specific vision to implement exactly where we were since it fell under Brandon's authority. Plus, there was the added benefit of leading affluent people, which would come in handy when confronting poverty. A move wasn't even on our radar, so consequently, our teaching started taking on this new shape. And it didn't sit well. Not that we encountered outright hostility, exactly. It was more like trying to press a square peg into a round hole. It just didn't match.

As we found ourselves unable to gain any traction, Easter snuck up on us. The day that changed everything.

Deeply moved by Shane Claiborne, among others, Brandon sent him an e-mail through dubious channels, basically telling him that *The Irresistible Revolution* was messing his wife up, and now he was reading it and didn't know what to do with it in his context. But, Brandon told him, we were wrestling with and asking new questions, so that was probably good. He just wanted Shane to know that his message mattered to a pastor in the suburbs, even if it was driving us crazy.

E-mail sent and forgotten.

Ring-ring-ring. "Hi, is this Brandon? This is Shane Claiborne . . . yes, it is . . . oh, I got your number off your e-mail . . . no, your wife is not involved in this . . . Anyway, I'm going to be speaking at a small Asian-American church in Austin Easter night, and I thought maybe we could have coffee afterward . . . no, you're not being punked . . . okay, I'll see you in a couple of days."

Seriously? Who does that? I get e-mails from strangers all the time, and I was feeling good about responding to them. But pilfering their numbers off their signature line and scheduling coffees with them when I come to their cities . . . Wow!

Anyhow, there was a 100 percent chance that coffee was happening, so we cleared Easter evening to spend with Shane and the members of Vox Veniae. (Check out this cool church at www.voxveniae.com—if I could, I would eat its website.)

Easter weekend, we blew the six services out of the water at our church: a big, incredible, fantastic production; guest musicians; "When the Saints Go Marching In"; trumpets; lights; gospel singers; rappers; sweet videography. Killer. We herded approximately ten billion people in and out of there like cattle, clearing them out as fast as possible before the next service. As far as "wow" factors go, no one left disappointed. You got it, Jack. And Jackie.

Fast-forward a few hours later: We changed into jeans and drove downtown for Vox Veniae's one little Easter service with their guest speaker, Shane Claiborne. The church rented this crappy space on the University of Texas campus, and we parked in a ramshackle parking lot a block away. As we walked up to the church, we saw a homeless-looking guy with weird hair, wearing what appeared to be a burlap sack in the shape of pants and a tunic. This was, of course, Shane. (He's been escorted out of several churches before they realized he was their guest speaker. Claiborne: Making Deacons Feel Awkward since 1998.)

There were maybe 150 people at this Easter service. It was simple and stripped down. Candles, an unscripted welcome. The worship was unself-conscious and pure, three or four guys in the band. It was completely unproduced and humble, all of it. It smacked of regular people and simple church; their only preoccupation was this obsession with Jesus. It was tangible. I loved every molecule of it. I wanted to sell my house and move into this room.

Toward the end of Shane's talk, he mentioned his time that morning with a large homeless community in San Antonio. He had asked their spokesman what their main needs were. Above all else, they needed good shoes. (The homeless community has chronic leg and back pain from long days standing in inadequate shoes.) He explained how they were on their feet all day, and the shoes they got from shelters and Goodwill were everyone else's castoffs, worn down, worn out.

As we were about to take Communion, Shane said, "You are under no coercion, but if you want to, you can leave your shoes at the altar when you take Communion. Oh! And leave your socks, too. We'll wash them and deliver them to the homeless community in San Antonio tomorrow."

Two significant particulars: one, Easter 2007 in Austin was unseasonably, crazy cold. Like thirty-one degrees that morning cold. Understand that in a typical April in Austin, we would all be wearing shorts and flip-flops. Guaranteed. From the youngest to the oldest. As it was, every person there had on real, substantial shoes because it was freezing outside.

Two, Brandon and I looked down at our shoes in unison and just started laughing. (Well, he laughed, and I cried.) Why? We were both wearing the brand-new cowboy boots we'd given each other for Christmas. By a huge margin, they were the most prized and expensive shoes we'd ever owned. I loved them so much that I gave them their own special box in my closet where moth and rust could not destroy.

Having thrown myself into this arena for a few months, I thought I would be thrilled to rip those boots off my rich feet and give them over to the homeless (who would promptly sell them since they are entirely impractical and worth a pretty penny—I've learned a few things). But I was discouraged to feel the twinge of selfishness rear its head first. *Seriously? I'm going to make a deal over boots? Have I come only this far, God? I stink.*

Jesus, unwilling to entertain my melodrama, cut to the chase: "Give them up. I have something to teach you." Evidently, this moment was not about me and my urban cowgirl boots. So I took them off, raised them to my lips for a farewell kiss—oh, okay, and an embrace—and Brandon and I left them at the altar along with our socks and the last remaining thread of reluctance.

I'll not do the moment justice, but at the close of the service, I watched all these smiling people gladly walk barefooted out into the cold, and I heard Jesus whisper, "This is how I want My church to look. I want her to rip the shoes off her feet for the suffering every single chance she gets. I want an altar full of socks and shoes right next to the Communion table. I want to see solidarity with the poor. I want true community rallied around My gospel. I want you and Brandon to figure out what it means to be a barefooted church."

A barefooted church.

It was so profound that we couldn't talk about it for two days.

(Oh? And Shane was so swarmed after the service that we slipped out so he wouldn't feel rushed and obligated to meet with us. At eleven thirty-five that night: ring-ring-ring. "It's Shane. Where did you go? Let's meet for breakfast before I leave town." That guy is the real deal. His life brings complete integrity to his message.)

Brandon's Take

At this point, we knew we were on a journey like never before. It was marked by a shift in thinking. Initially, it wasn't about strategy or methodology; it was about our personal hearts and affections. God was speaking to us as never before. Let me add a little perspective to what Jen said about our Easter turnaround.

Mind you, over two days I had worked six Easter services at my church. They were massive, full of energy, and exciting. We had the highest attendance in the history of our church. And I was *tired*. So tired that I almost stayed home that night instead of driving downtown with Jen to Vox Veniae. But since we had committed to grabbing coffee with Shane afterward, I decided to go anyway. Glad I did.

During worship, I was really giving it up. You know when you're so tired that you feel a bit vulnerable? And in the middle of a David Crowder song, I had a vision (or a daydream . . . depending on your theology—wink).

Whatever it was, in it I saw myself walking down the west campus street just outside the church we were in, and a homeless guy yelled from the sidewalk, "Hey, give me your boots."

As an excuse not to give up my boots, my immediate imaginary response was, "They won't fit you!"

To which he replied, "Oh, they'll fit."

And that was it. I was confused. "What do you want me to do with this, God? Am I supposed to walk down Guadalupe Street after the service? Am I gonna see this guy? Whatever it is, God, I'll do it. I've asked You to speak to me, so I'll listen."

It was settled. Afterward, I would walk down the street, find that guy, and hand over my boots. I'd explain it to Jen later. Of course, as you read earlier, I couldn't have been more surprised when we were given the opportunity to leave our shoes for the homeless during Communion. Thirty minutes after that vision, I was handed a chance to obey it. *In church*.

I was overwhelmed. I guess that homeless guy was right. They'll fit someone.

God had spoken loudly and very personally. "Yes, Brandon, I'm in this."

Jen and I both were very convinced. This was for real. So we began the journey of figuring out what this new kind of life looked like. Honestly, I was loving it. The experiences were reshaping my heart, and I could tell I was being transformed. The challenge would surely be to get other Christ followers to experience the same journey, to take the focus off themselves and place it on others, specifically on the least of these. That would be my job.

I began to pray about how to apply it. I felt the best solution was to take "mission" from the final stage of our spiritual development process and place it under "discipleship." It had to be a key element. It needed to become an integrated part of our lives—maybe even a discipline like daily Bible study was—not just an event we did once a year.

But something was missing. As I met with my leaders and cast the vision, it was obvious our zeal was not the same. I didn't feel as though God was going before me with the same power I had experienced. It wasn't falling on entirely deaf ears; it just seemed to lack substance. My leadership seemed so void of His presence that I found myself in my office in prayer, literally weeping, asking God, "What am I doing wrong? Why is this not taking root? What do You want me to do?"

Then the answer came. Probably the one I didn't want to hear at the time: "Brandon, this vision is not for here. There's already a vision here. I'm giving you a new one."

My heart and mind immediately conceded as if they already knew. "Okay, God, show me what that means."

Over the next few weeks, God affirmed His calling to leave all that I had known. I hoped, and even expected, that He'd explain how that calling would manifest before we stepped away. I begged Him for that. But He was silent. That summer I discovered the journey was not only about something new but also about being willing to go, even before we knew where we were going.

NEW

Clarity was starting to crack through. Over the next few weeks, it dawned on us that this wasn't a new program for our current placement. This wasn't a gear change in the same car. Instead, this was something new. I mean really new. New, as in a new place for us. New, as in Brandon was going to have a new role. New, as in "catch a clue, Hatmakers; I've been getting you ready. Unbeknownst to you, I've already given you your vision. Go be a barefooted church." (Insert hyperventilation.)

The what, the where, the how? Adorably, God wasn't yet ready to deal in those specifics. The question on the table to us was, "Will you go?" The answer we put back was, "Yes." That was enough trauma for the month of May, thank you. The mere knowledge that (1) telling, (2) leaving, and (3) starting over were in our immediate future sent us to the fetal position.

There was no way around this—that was certain. We saw a tunnel of chaos in our future, and we were headed straight for it. (As I write this, I can still feel the ropes of anxiety and fear that snaked around us back then. We knew a clean path through this transition was nonexistent. That May we prayed a lot for the Rapture.)

However, ignoring this call was not an option. Jesus already hammered that excuse in the sheep and goats story:

> He will say to those on his left, "Depart from me, you who are cursed, into the eternal fire prepared for the devil and his angels. For I was hungry and you gave me nothing to eat, I was thirsty and you gave me nothing to drink, I was a stranger and you did not invite me in, I needed clothes and you did not clothe me, I was sick and in prison and you did not look after me."
> They also will answer, "Lord, when did we see you hungry or thirsty or a stranger or needing clothes or sick or in prison, and did not help you?"
> He will reply, "Truly I tell you, whatever you did not do for one of the least of these, you did not do for me." (Matthew 25:41-45)

Never once did Jesus charge them with something they did wrong. His entire indictment was on what they didn't do right.

It was a sin of neglect, a crime of omission. And it went far beyond ignoring poverty. Jesus explained that when we ignore the least, we ignore Him. No amount of spinning or clever justification can neutralize Jesus' point. If we claim affinity for Christ but turn a blind eye to those He identified Himself with, there is no honor in that. There is no truth in it.

This is how grave the gospel's challenge is: "Whatever you did for one of the least of these brothers and sisters of mine, you did for me" (Matthew 25:40). It is as simple as it is radical. If every believer obeyed accordingly, I daresay we could confront all that ails society.

These are the words by which we are sent, but wondrously, they are also the words by which we are saved. They are not simply a revelation of crisis and the call to active love; they are also an invitation to personal recognition. Each one of us, as it turns out, counts as the least. We all bear the image of Christ, no matter how devalued we feel. As poet and Jesuit priest Gerard Manley Hopkins wrote, "Christ plays in ten thousand places, lovely in limbs and lovely in eyes not his."[1]

Ultimately, it is not nation or race, church or citizenship that gives people value. It is not sinlessness or innocence that makes us precious. It is not that Jesus looks on us as helpless or powerful, poor or rich, weak or strong. We are loved because we are living images of God, made in His likeness and created for the heights of His glory and the depths of communion. Our very God took on our form for the love of humanity, privilege or poverty aside. In contrast to God's perfection, we are all the least, each and every one, identified entirely with a Savior who loves us recklessly. This parable reveals as much about the character of God as it does about the course of human affairs.

Miraculously, there will come a day when we stand before God Almighty with nothing but this human life standing up on our behalf, full of failure and omissions. And just when all hope is lost, when we have nothing left to hold out, nothing to show God, no more to demonstrate our worthiness with, the Son will step in, in all His glory and righteousness, and say to the Father, "Whatever you do to the least of these, these brothers and sisters of Mine, you do unto Me."

So this Matthew 25 passage—in its greatest depth—is not merely a moral challenge or judgment on this world. Nor is it just a program for social action or poverty reduction. Rather, it describes the mystery of salvation that grounds all hierarchy, motivates all action, and makes possible the acceptance of our identity as redeemed sinners.

Resisting the urge to plagiarize, I'll quote (and cite!) Richard Rohr one last time:

> The Gospels say very clearly that God loves imperfect things. But it's only the imperfect and the broken who can believe that. Those who don't have anything to prove or protect can believe that they are loved as they are. But we who have spent our lives ascending the spiritual ladder have a harder time hearing the truth. For the truth isn't found up at the top, but down at the bottom. And by trying to climb

the ladder we miss Christ, who comes down through the Incarnation.[2]

For the bread of God is he who comes down from heaven and gives life to the world. (John 6:33, ESV)

Heavy Influences—Phase Three

- The homeless community of Austin
- ARCH: Austin Resource Center for the Homeless (www.frontsteps.org)
- Shane Claiborne
- The Barna Group
- *Boiling Point* by George Barna and Mark Hatch
- *Same Kind of Different as Me* by Ron Hall and Denver Moore

PHASE FOUR: FINDING YOUR TRIBE

We see a church that is driven by God's vision for unity to be bold and innovative in partnering across denominations with other churches, ministries, and organizations. We believe that together we can share the good news of Jesus Christ with a hurting world regardless of social status, ethnicity, or faith background.

VALUE:
*Partnering with others to make a
difference in our community and world.*

KEY SCRIPTURE:
Isaiah 58

OFF THE PLATFORM

In 2008, Brandon and I made it to our fifteenth anniversary. GLORY AND EXULTATIONS! Considering that we married as infants and listed as our first annual joint income $11,237 for the entire year of 1994, it's something of a celebration that we made it that far. When people wax nostalgic over their early years of wedded bliss, I am certain they never lived in a decrepit seventy-year-old house where they could see their breath in the master bedroom during the winter, while living on peanut butter toast and dreaming about the day they could fill their whole tank up with gas rather than spend $2.10 in dimes. That said, we rewarded our longevity with an anniversary cruise to Alaska, making the brilliant decision to take our best friends and leave behind the children. Coincidentally, we received the unexpected reward of being labeled "the young people" on the ship, which was infinitely superior to competing with spring breakers in bikinis in Jamaica. Plus, in Alaska we got to wear fat-people clothes and didn't have to diet beforehand. Win-win.

As an excursion, the six of us booked a zip-line course through the rainforest in Ketchikan. On the waiver was this condition: "Minimum weight is ninety pounds for the rainforest canopy and zip-line expedition"—uh, the last time I weighed ninety pounds was in seventh grade—"and maximum weight is 250. Weight limits are established to ensure proper zipping speed on the courses."

All of us were safely within these boundaries except for our friend Tray, proud former offensive lineman for the Alabama Crimson Tide, standing six foot four and comfortably north of the 250-pound mark. We read the fine print to determine if fudging his numbers would simply result in increased velocity or something more serious like his tragic death as he plunged to the rainforest floor. Hoping for the former, his wife, Jenny, confirmed (read: lied about) the necessary weight requirements on the waiver.

As it turned out, the zip line was a little scary. Okay, we freaked out. We were 135 feet up in the trees, where our zip-line platforms were secured with duct tape and hot glue. All of us, including our twenty-four-year-old guide, Chad, were to zip from one platform to the next, harnessed in by skinny little ribbons and a silver buckle or two.

"Sit back into your harness and drop off the edge of the platform," instructed Chad nonchalantly, as if we were two feet off the ground. "It is your responsibility to slow down by pulling on the cable as you approach the next platform." That we were somehow responsible for our own well-being seemed fairly ridiculous, and we felt certain one of us would be dead before nightfall.

Here is when we discovered the meaning of the phrase "Weight limits are established to ensure proper zipping speed on the courses." As we reached the eight-hundred-foot-long "Ben's revenge," the longest and steepest zip line of the course, our lying ways caught up to us. Tray, acting on intuition and a basic understanding of physics, said, "This feels like a bad idea." He stood there for some time, as we all did, not wanting him to die but certainly willing to sacrifice him rather than perish in the treetops.

Chad hollered from the next platform, where he stood ready to receive each adventurer, "Come on, Tray!" So without further ado, Tray dropped off that platform and promptly turned into a speeding freight train, his "zipping speed" no longer *ensured* or *proper*. His momentum was so alarming that from about the three-hundred-foot mark, Chad started cussing. The closer Tray got, the lower Chad got, attempting a lineman's stance to break a landing that surely became legendary in the state of Alaska.

When Tray hit that platform with the velocity of a large

speeding bullet, he knocked down the landing stairs as if they were matchsticks and flattened poor undersized Chad against the tree like a panini sandwich, knocking the wind violently out of them both. Trying to be helpful, the rest of us fell down on the platform and screamed with laughter for twenty minutes. Chad earned his paycheck that day, which I'm sure he used on his cracked ribs.

The zip line was the highlight of our trip, but stepping off that first platform and enduring a brief free fall were really scary, harder than we expected. It turned out to be exhilarating, but departing from the safety of the stand was terrifying—though our guide was urging us to do it.

Leaving is hard, even when a great adventure awaits you.

By the end of May, we knew we were leaving our church. To go where? We didn't have the first inkling. That was somewhere out there, yet to be determined. What lay in front of us was the telling, the transition, leaving the platform. After seven years, there was no doubt: This would be tough.

Brandon told our pastor in early June; we left in August. I hardly know what to say except that this season was terribly hard. I wish I had some of those weeks back to rethink this conversation or better word that piece of correspondence. We navigated with pure intentions and a fierce desire to do this well.

But things like leaving, new ideas, and perception—further complicated by no details about where we were going—made for a difficult transition. No one wanted the particulars more than Brandon and me, but part of our task was going without knowing. Those were hard, difficult days. Sometimes following God is the worst. I can say with some confidence: if you go wherever God says and when, expect to be misunderstood.

And go anyway.

ON A NEED-TO-KNOW BASIS

We entertained every ministry option: planting a church, pastoring an existing church, serving as pastor of missions at another church in town, joining the nonprofit sector, becoming hippie radicals. Our single desire was to find the context where we could become the barefooted church of our dreams, and no option was off-limits.

Although God's silence was maddening, I see the important role it played. There is the obvious reason: a faith exercise. God has a history of behaving this way when calling people to a holy task. To Abraham: Go to a place I will show you. I mean I'll show you *later* after you leave. To Moses: Go to Pharaoh and liberate My people. Oh? Just tell him "I Am" sent you. To Isaiah: Go stripped and barefooted for three years. Just do it; it will mean something later.

I wonder how their stories would have gone had they possessed clear directives at their launch. If they had understood the final picture at the beginning, then every detour, every setback, every unexpected turn could have derailed their mission. Had Abraham known that Canaan was, well, occupied, it might have affected his resolve to get there. Or if Moses had known that forty years of homelessness would commence after their liberation, he might have been softer with Pharaoh. If Isaiah had realized he'd never see Israel's restoration, his prophecies could have lost their thunder.

For us, it was essential that our dream of becoming a barefooted church was primary; how that materialized was a distant second. Otherwise, we would have held too tightly to the method, the details, the strategy. We are Type-As; it is our way. Had we become enmeshed with our specific task, there would have been much cause to doubt it in this early season. We were unprepared for the opposition and angst, and had we possessed a clear vision, we would have defiled with defensiveness something God intended to be pure.

Perhaps this applies to you, too, good reader. God may be leading you away without a clear final destination yet. As maddening as that is, could it be that He needs you to release *what was* before you can appropriately grasp *what will be*? Could it be that you might accidentally squash the lovely vision if you obtain it too soon? There is a horrid beauty in following God slightly blind. The victory later is sweeter, the prize more valuable than breath. Obviously, we are Americans; we like a plan, we like assurances. But the ways of faith exist so far outside of our tidy boundaries, it is a wonder we can ever receive its mysteries at all.

As it was, we could only hold loosely to something we didn't even understand, and that put us in a position of faith and terrible humility. We can wreck the spirit of a mission by prematurely focusing on the strategy. When the "how" eclipses the "why" too soon, we create a positional shift to defend and execute rather than listen and receive. Once clear territory is staked, we turn into guards, protecting our decisions.

This is certainly my bent, so mercifully I had nothing to defend when backed into a corner. I will take it on the chin only if I have no other options, so that's probably why we were removed from our post before receiving a single helpful detail about what to do next. God was unwilling to let us spoil this splendid undertaking, so He didn't explain it until we could safely receive it without ruining it.

Which turned out to be a no-job, no-church, no-salary scenario.

Since we couldn't rely on our default responses—planning, organizing, mobilizing, controlling—we did the only thing left: We prayed like crazy people. We prayed for vision; for like-minded partners; for mentors; for a salary; for unity, strength, healing, courage, clarity; for opportunities; for resources. Did I mention we prayed for a salary? Never have we stood with such open hands, clinging to nothing, ready for anything.

I hate that place and love it—depends on the day. There is a freedom in not being in control, when something utterly imagined by God is coming for you. It's exciting and sort of awful. It felt as if we were on the precipice of a violent waterfall and our raft had gotten sideways. My instincts told me to bail, but this was the most crucial moment to stay the course. I was learning how to release, to not defend myself, to not act as my own protector.

I asked a lot of "why" questions that had no answers. In his book *When God Doesn't Make Sense*, James Dobson wrote,

> A better question becomes "Why does it matter?"
> It is not your responsibility to explain what God is doing with your life. He has not provided enough information to figure it out. Instead, you are asked to turn loose and let God be God. Therein lies the secret to the "peace that transcends understanding."[1]

Turning loose is part of preferring the bottom; it's an unexpected front door to peace. But it is legitimately hard. It requires conscious decisions to abandon formerly vital things like reputation, perception, position, control. And make no mistake: if you begin to value a lower life, you will be misinterpreted and likely criticized. Most people don't want American staples like comfort and safety and prosperity challenged. Your instincts will say, "Defend and protect or possibly abandon ship," but that is the worst internal advice ever. Don't listen to yourself. You can lose it all—all the things you

JEN HATMAKER

thought mattered most—and rise up to tell a better story yet. Turn it loose.

This was probably our most important lesson, more valuable than the specifics we would later engage, because it's easy to visit the bottom with works while our hearts remain higher up. That's just charity. It's a moment, not a permanent relocation. It is something entirely different to adopt the mind of Christ. That's when we don't just act lowly; we are lowly. Our minds are not safely secured up higher, awaiting our return after we're done patronizing those at the bottom.

The decisions you make in a low position are completely opposite those made in a high place. The people you seek counsel from are different. The leaders you expose yourself to are different. The way you move forward is different. There are top-dwelling rules that are irrelevant at the bottom, and you're free from adhering to them. It's not just a positional change that affects you today; it informs every decision and relationship in your future.

This is probably why it wasn't until we were lying on the ground that God delivered our task and vision. I shudder to imagine how we would have destroyed that dream had we possessed it when we were higher up. Not a single decision would have had any integrity. We were so unprepared to receive our mission until the second we did. When we had nothing left to protect, no position left to defend, no reputation left to guard, and no one else to please, we got our marching orders.

FREE

We weren't to pastor an existing church, although that had the benefit of, well, benefits and stuff. We weren't to pioneer another church's mission initiative, though that tempting offer was on the table. We hadn't been interrupted to start a nonprofit benefiting our favorite people group, although that had the added incentive of not being a church. (Sometimes church is really obnoxious.)

No, our mission was to start a new church in our beloved city—roughly 93 percent unchurched or dechurched—from scratch. We had not a dime, supporter, mentor, or plan. This was the phase when God became the hero that He is. For the way He stepped in with such dramatic provision, I am in awe of His sovereignty; we couldn't have invented this route.

We'd been on our own for twelve days when a mysterious ally called.

"Brandon, we got your name from a guy who knew a guy who went to see a man about a horse"—or something like that—"and I'd like to meet you. I'm Dennis Jeffery, superintendent of the Rocky Mountain Conference for the Free Methodists."

First obvious question: What the heck is a Free Methodist? And why is he calling us from Denver? What a happy time in the story. Picture the best human you know: That is Dennis Jeffery to us. (Months later, when we joined Dennis in San Diego for a conference, we asked about dress code for dinner, and he said, "I'm wearing a Hawaiian bowling shirt." We adore him for his giant heart, not his fashion sense.) Dennis is the pastor of everyone's dreams, the one who loves without agenda or pretense, at all times, in every way. I don't think he has ever sinned. Once I thought he might, but instead he said, "Well, rats," like an endearing citizen from 1953.

You have likely not heard of the Free Methodists because they've been quietly doing global ministry since 1860, when they split from the main Methodist conference over racial inequality. Not only that, churches had developed a nasty habit of charging congregants for preferred seating; the more you paid, the closer you sat. Poor people were relegated to the back, often pushed out altogether by paying members. Convinced that people and church attendance should be *free*, the Free Methodist church was born.

Quoting his mentor Stephen Olin, B. T. Roberts, the founder of the Free Methodist church, wrote,

> There are hot controversies about the true Church. What constitutes it, what is essential to it? . . . Does a church preach the gospel to the poor—preach it effectively? Does it convert and sanctify the people? . . . If not, we need not take the trouble of asking any more questions about it. It has missed the main matter. . . .
>
> Friends of Jesus . . . the Gospel is committed to your trust. . . . You are to dig for rough diamonds amid the ruins of fallen humanity, and polish them up for jewels in the crown of your Redeemer. The church edifice is your workshop. Do not, we beseech you, convert it into a show room, to display, not the graces of Christians, but the vain fashions of the world.[1]

With their dedication to mission and racial parity, early Free Methodists were found in black and mixed congregations; on mission fields in India, Africa, and China; and later in rescue missions in US cities. They insisted on simple buildings and plain dress on Sundays so the poor would feel comfortable among them. (How wonderful.)

Because of that trajectory, about three-fourths of their congregants are in developing countries today. Free Methodist churches are modestly represented in the United States, but if you live in Burundi, Africa, take your pick: There are 821 organized Free Methodist churches with a combined membership of nearly 100,000 locals. (Increase this by the eighty other countries the Free Methodist church calls home.) They have remained a faithful sect on the margins, holding fast to the fiery teachings of John Wesley while rejecting the trappings that would distract from their mission.

The target demographic for the Free Methodist church was explained in *The Earnest Christian* in 1860:

> At times they are tremblingly alive to the fact that a religion of fashion and parade, of pomp and show, and circumstance, cannot save their souls. The Holy Ghost presses home the truth that Christ's disciples are characterized by self denial, humility, and love.
>
> It is for this increasing class of persons that we write.[2]

Their mission included one other primary group:

> The claims of the neglected poor, the class to which Christ and the Apostles belonged, the class for whose special benefit the Gospel was designed, to all the ordinances of Christianity, will be advocated with all the candor and ability we can command. In order that the masses, who have a peculiar claim to the Gospel of Christ may be reached, the necessity of plain churches, with the seats free, of plainness of

dress, of spirituality and simplicity in worship, will, we trust, be set forth with convincing arguments.[3]

To this day, Free Methodist churches, by their posture and passions, attract two types of people: believers hungry for the straight-up gospel—simple in presentation, powerful in expression—and the marginalized who need good news in the form of salvation, assistance, and Christian fellowship. This has always been their particular limb in the body of Christ, an extremity, perhaps, but no less vital than more conspicuous parts of the body.

It's the limb of the bare feet.

Dennis Jeffery called us because the Free Methodist conference was developing a church-planting initiative in several heavily influential US cities, starting with Austin, Texas—home of the mighty longhorns, The Salt Lick Barbecue, and the Hatmaker family, recently called to build a barefooted church targeting hungry believers ready to live on mission in this very city but with no resources to do it. Not only were the Free Methodists prepared to fund this effort, they had mobilized a prayer team of sixty people who'd been interceding diligently for the new church in Austin since January, the same month I asked God to raise up a holy passion in me. Another key family was already on the ground, preparing for the church and asking God to call their pastor forward.

I don't mean to ruin the suspense, but it was us.

Barely two weeks after we hit the pavement, the following prayers were answered: complete funding effective immediately, a core team already in place, pastoral mentorship in the form of a Hawaiian-bowling-shirt–wearing saint and others like him, prayer cover, vision, a *perfectly* matched partnership in the work of the church, and overwhelming relief that not only were we no longer alone, we were part of something inspiring and beautiful and much larger than the scope of our reach.

This revived our dream for unity among churches. What we need more than denominational or invented boundaries is a commitment to do the work of Christ together. Church, we are on the same team. What is good for the kingdom is good for us all and cause for great celebration. In our prayers for harmony, answers came in the form of several denominations that said, "We want some skin in this game." We are spiritually and financially supported by Free Methodists, the Bible Church, the Baptists, and nondenominational congregations. When people ask what we are, we kind of shrug and say, "Cross-denominational?" We invented that. You can borrow it.

It is remarkable to witness different denominations coming together across party lines, beyond doctrinal differences, and past local territorialism to help birth a new church for the sake of the kingdom. We signed paperwork with Free Methodist leaders from Denver in the offices of the Austin Baptist Association, and Brandon immediately enrolled in a training course for church planters through Hill Country Bible Church. How's that for unheard of?

ISAIAH, ALAN, AND ME

Now that we had the skeleton, it was time to hang some meat on the bones. It reminded me of my friend Stephanie, who teaches first grade at an affluent school in Austin. During the first week of classes, a concerned father cornered her and asked, "What are you doing to prepare my son for Yale?" Quick on her feet and not in the mood for intimidation, Stephanie answered, "Well, first I'm going to teach him to stop picking his nose and eating the plunder. Next on the list is walking in a straight line for more than five seconds. I'll be ready to write a recommendation to Yale by the end of the year, I'm sure."

When you're six, fixating on Yale is somewhat premature.

When your church is eight seconds old, fancy things like services and tithe checks remain somewhere in Futureland too. It takes a lot of work to prep the surface, and this was about when we realized we had no idea how to start a church from scratch. What do we do first? How do we stay true to the vision? It was overwhelming, and I complicated matters by operating in an emotional drift. My mental space was consumed with loss from our departure, and I could not find center. I wanted to embrace the adventure, but leaving the platform was all I could think about.

That fall, I facilitated a study of Isaiah with twelve women on our church-planting team. By the way, a church planter without a committed team of laborers is doomed. The combined effect of the few hours a week each partner invested is the reason I'm not writing a book on a church-plant failure. Anyway, our intent was to read a chapter a day for sixty-six straight days until we were through Isaiah. However, we were derailed by the rather depressing repetitions in the first half of the book. (The only buzzkill worse than Isaiah was Jesus.) So after thirteen same-sounding chapters, summed up like this . . .

God: You people are like an open sore.
Israel: Who, us?
God: Yes. I want to murder every last one of you.

. . . we skipped from chapter 13 to chapter 40, where the restoration part started. As I needed both healing and vision,

I gorged on these passages like I had never eaten solid food. I embodied Jeremiah's sentiment: "When your words came, I ate them" (Jeremiah 15:16). I could not wait for my daily dose of Isaiah; it was wreaking good havoc with me.

Cut to a momentous day in the story. One November morning, I'd received one of those middle-school-type reports when one friend tells you what another "friend" said behind your back. Only it wasn't about boyfriends and school dances; these words slandered my integrity and honor, disparaging our little church and my very heart. Spoken to people I love. *Devastated* is not a strong enough word to describe my reaction. That was a dark morning. I was ready for fight or flight, but I knew I couldn't stay in emotional purgatory for another day.

That same evening, we'd already scheduled our first "truck run" with Alan Graham, founder of Mobile Loaves & Fishes. (This organization takes fully loaded trucks with food, drinks, clothes, and supplies to the forsaken parts of Austin to feed the homeless and working poor. To date, it has fed more than a million people.) After an evening in shameful day-rate motels structured to take advantage of desperate people by offering them deplorable living conditions, I was emotionally wrung out.

All night, Alan had shown us how to love genuinely, without condescension or patronization, pity or permissiveness. Every person received a full-body hug from him, a word of peace and love, his phone number, dignity. It was beautiful, and I learned more from six hours with Alan than six years sitting in a church pew. (Plus he looks like Santa with the added entertainment of a teeny cursing habit.)

Late that night, while we were eating delicioso Mexican food with Alan, he started probing about our embryonic church plant. Still so fragile, we sort of stammered through our dream of becoming a barefooted church. Alan began speaking prophetically about church and life, boiling it down to its basic essence: "Brandon and Jen, our mission as believers is so simple: Base everything on Matthew 25"—my life-changing chapter!—"and Isaiah 58."

Wait, what? That's my chapter to study tomorrow.

The next morning, raw from bearing witness to that magical place where mercy meets poverty, I got up early to devour Isaiah 58, understanding instinctively that God had been steadily working toward this moment.

> Day after day they seek me out;
>> they seem eager to know my ways,
> as if they were a nation that does what is right
>> and has not forsaken the commands of its God.
>> (verse 2)

I realize God was talking about Israel, but most American Christians have substituted the United States as God's current chosen nation. Allow me to mention that we have no special claims to God's protection or provision. There was one chosen branch; the rest of us are only wild olive shoots grafted in by faith, not nationality. With the resurrection of

Jesus and the salvation of humanity, we are no longer identified by nation, race, gender, or any group dynamic. We don't get to stand behind the shield of church or denomination or political party. There is no "us" and "them" anymore.

"Us" is the worldwide assembly of the rescued who have been transformed from hopeless humans to adopted sons and daughters of God through faith in Jesus. The end. Our group identification has nothing to do with where we were born or who we were born to. As Americans, we cannot act contrary to God's Word and His will yet expect His blessings. You know what God would say? "As if they were a nation that does what is right and has not forsaken the commands of its God." As if.

IGNORANCE IS NOT BLISS

They ask me for just decisions
    and seem eager for God to come near them.
"Why have we fasted," they say,
    "and you have not seen it?
Why have we humbled ourselves,
    and you have not noticed?" (Isaiah 58:2-3)

If there was one pitfall we wanted to avoid, it was becoming a church that places programs above people or the desire for the sweet spirit of Christ. A growing church can quickly become distracted with the necessary business of things and miss the whole point, even annihilate the point, jeopardizing its DNA along the way.

This temptation isn't exclusive to church. If all of us are not careful, priorities can shift to chasing growth or success at all costs. It is our nature to get consumed by ambitious leadership and bottom lines, where secular business tactics become necessary to maintain momentum, much less thrive. These all increase our risk of being pulled away from the countercultural manner of Christ. It makes it harder to stay in the wake of God, not easier; this is true corporately as the church and personally as Christ followers. Then if God's hand is removed—shock, confusion. Wait? Weren't we doing everything You wanted? Why haven't You noticed?

Aware of this, King David constantly invited God to search his heart and the hidden motives within as he led the nation of Israel. The only thing worse than being ignorant is being ignorant of our own ignorance, when we don't even know what we don't know. What we do know is that "the heart is deceitful" and can fool even its owner.[1] Much damage can be inflicted from that place. We are easily distracted, losing perspective and reacting desperately, but no circumstance gives us license to discard the essentials: love, mercy, compassion, justice. The means do not justify the end when it comes to God's kingdom. *The means are everything;* the end is secondary. We don't obtain godly results through selfishness, greed, corruption, ruthlessness; not through lying, misrepresenting, dividing, slandering; nor though neglect, apathy, ego, pride. If these patterns drive the manner in which we get from here to there, I don't care what it looks like when the dust settles; it's garbage.

God is unimpressed by a spiritual veneer or our business savvy, either as a faith community or individually as Christ followers. None of us gets to treat people like expendable articles and expect God to look the other way because it somehow advanced His kingdom or had nothing to do with it. We can't ignore God's ways and expect to maintain His favor. We don't get to neglect the major values of the gospel and claim preference or context. The demands of church leadership—and, more importantly, of *living our lives*—never come with a permission slip to act contrary to our heritage in Christ.

> Yet on the day of your fasting, you do as you please
>   and exploit all your workers.
> Your fasting ends in quarreling and strife,
>   and in striking each other with wicked fists.
> You cannot fast as you do today
>   and expect your voice to be heard on high.
>   (Isaiah 58:3-4)

Expect to be ignored.

That sums up God's opinion rather completely. Not only was God the discarded lover in this scenario, wounded and heartbroken, but He had attached His name to these people. They were the branch chosen to represent the one True God for all the world to see. Not only did they reject Him, they defiled His reputation and delayed His fame. Though God desired the redemption of all nations, *no* nation had reason to be attracted to the God of Israel; all they saw was the constant hypocrisy of Yahweh's people.

Does our duplicitous representation of Jesus not only assault Him but also offend the rest of the world? Is this partly why the church is declining in America? How could it not be? When we strike others on the same day we fast, we bring no integrity to the gospel. Unbelievers may not understand the nuances of our theology, but they know acting holy while injuring and offending others is repulsive. We shouldn't expect our voices to be heard on high, and we had better get used to being ignored by people, too.

In *The Tangible Kingdom*, Hugh Halter and Matt Smay wrote,

> People in America are not ignorant of Christianity. They've heard the message, seen our churches on every corner, they flick by our Christian TV shows, they see our fish symbols on the backs of our cars. They've seen so much of pop Christian culture that they have a programmed response to us: *Ignore, ignore, ignore.* What's needed is a change of parameters—something that will alter their emotional response.[2]

At the conception of our church, some of the first questions we asked were: "Why aren't people compelled by the church anymore?" "Why is the church so easily ignored when we're supposed to be the arm of Christ?" The "come to us" system is no longer an appropriate response to the paradigms that exist in our world. Presenting a kingdom alternative to the world is now imperative, but we must acknowledge the paradigm shift that has taken place.

A MODERN
MESS

You and I were born into modernism, a worldview launched during the enlightenment in the 1700s, when "the lights went on." Men were now governed by reason, intelligence, and scientific orientation. Knowledge was king, and people believed that through scientific discovery and human reasoning, they could know everything or figure it out. This period was marked by extreme confidence in human ability, respect of authority, clear rights and wrongs, and individual rights. Other modern ideas included:

- More education creates a moral society.
- We make decisions if they make logical sense.

- All knowledge is reachable via the mind.
- We can pull ourselves up by our bootstraps.
- People can only trust what is proven through observation and experimentation.
- Modernity deeply values security and protection.
- Influence is obtained through institutions, structures, and positioning. The higher up in the structure, the more power you have because modern people respect position.
- The needs of the individual supersede the needs of the community.[1]

While the list is certainly a reductionist explanation, that worldview dominated society for almost three hundred years. Naturally, modernism shaped the church; despite our efforts to remain above the influence of society, our beliefs are so ingrained with the prevailing paradigm that we're unaware how entrenched we actually are. Modern themes have affected the church in many ways:

- We understand Christianity through factual research, based on an unshakable foundation of absolute truth.
- Apologetics (defending the faith) is a primary tool for evangelism.
    - This tactic can be employed completely void of a relational context.
- Christianity is about "Jesus and me." He is my "personal Lord and Savior." I accept Him while

everyone's head is bowed and I can raise my hand in private. Community involvement is optional because this is a personal decision.

- • We come to Christ through a logical, measurable decision: "I walked the aisle when I was nine after hearing the facts and making the choice."
- • Christians make decisions based on how they feel God is speaking to them personally; it has little to do with community.
- • The modern value of security is deeply rooted in minimizing risk, pulling our kids and families completely out of their cultural context, and avoiding a missional lifestyle.
- • Pastors expect people to respect them simply for their position as "church leader."[2]

This is the worldview I grew up in. My (toxic) evangelistic strategy was (1) prove, (2) defend, and (3) put someone to the question. If she couldn't follow the logical steps 1 through 8 as outlined in my helpful Christian tract, then her heart was hardened. I could only hope Jesus didn't come back before she came to her senses.

I spent most of my time figuring out how to "be separate" (2 Corinthians 6:17), but what with my arrogance and judgment, I'm not sure that was a tall order. I feared culture and the people in it, certain that my proximity to them would pave the road to perdition. Sadly, I took what my spiritual teachers said as hard facts, parroting their interpretations to the detriment of anyone who dared disagree. I didn't become a critical thinker until my late twenties. My understanding of discipleship was linear; there was an obvious path to maturity through progressive steps, not a journey of discovery that involved several factors at once. Ultimately, my faith was about me and my stuff, and the greater good of my community was simply not my problem.

From a modern standpoint, people come to church because they respect the institution and the pastor, they share a clear interpretation of right and wrong not up for discussion, it is a safe place to be sequestered, and you can navigate your faith without interference from others. Because of their resistance to cultural influence, many churches still function with modern values in a society that no longer agrees with the tenets of that paradigm.

And therein lies the crucial shift.

"TURN AND FACE THE STRANGE CH-CH-CHANGES"

In the last fifty years, Western culture has undergone a transition to postmodernity, which challenges everything the modern paradigm holds dear. The 1960s amped up a process that was already underway. Following the assassinations of Martin Luther King Jr., John F. Kennedy, and Robert F. Kennedy, many Americans began fearing that even our finest leaders were vulnerable despite their knowledge. The great progress of human rights might be reversed. Add the political chaos of the Vietnam War and the awareness that nuclear scientific advances could destroy us all, and people were questioning their faith in science in light of the catastrophic destruction it made possible.

Thus began a period of doubting authorities and deconstructing their carte blanche control over our society and collective consciousness.

Halter and Smay wrote,

> The government wasn't going to have authority over us, the church wasn't, the military wasn't, our parents weren't. It was a massive rebuttal to Western/ modern values. Because of this distrust of political, family, and church leaders, "personal preference," philosophical freedom, and relativism took center stage.[1]

The postmodern worldview questions whether facts are completely knowable and whether logic is really the best tool with which to navigate life. Truth is no longer objective, concrete, observable; it is subjective and dependent on circumstances.

For many postmoderns, the prominence of the individual is diminished. They say the personal pursuit of happiness should no longer be supreme; rather, the betterment of the community is a dominant value. Here are some other variances of postmodernity:

- Rationalism doesn't make a better society.
- Deconstruction reigns; there is no absolute truth that undergirds all of life.
- Everyone's story is part of a bigger narrative.

- Postmoderns ask questions and challenge the status quo.
- Postmoderns have a global outlook in terms of responsibility for the ecology of the earth and its inhabitants.
- Since most postmoderns do not believe in absolute truth, judging is preposterous.
- Postmoderns are marked by a deep skepticism, and the twin ideas of power and control are repulsive.
- Answers to life's questions are never simple or simply reduced. Postmoderns believe life is messy, not easily dissected or understood.[2]

Like most of my generation raised in church, I have a foot in both the modern and postmodern worldviews. Much of my lifestyle was shaped by modernity, even as I felt uncertain about its solubility. While promoting the logical path of discipleship, I privately questioned the style and effectiveness. Much tension came from applying my modern spiritual ideas to real life; despite its claims, this approach didn't solve every problem or win over every (or any) skeptic.

What kinds of churches are reaching postmoderns? Those turning the corner have adjusted accordingly, though it has little to do with style and more to do with posture. Vanguard churches twenty years ago swapped choirs for bands and suits for jeans, but reaching an increasingly postmodern society requires much deeper changes:

- Scripture is applied in context of the needs of the community.
- Relationships are of utmost importance.
  - Postmoderns frequently seek God in community rather than alone.
  - Discipleship occurs over years in community.
- Authenticity is everything; the appearance of being slick, packaged, or overproduced is suspect.
- Postmoderns have been burned by positional authorities (government, parents, church leaders), so they are suspicious of establishment and must be won over by integrity not title.
  - They do, however, value genuine moral authority.
- Evangelism no longer emphasizes the rational linear decision an individual makes at a specific point. It is a process, a journey, a story.
- Postmoderns are drawn to a church that guards against the effects of consumerism both on its members and itself.
- How genuinely a church engages relief work and the care of global society is everything to a postmodern.[3]

Modernism says, "I have all the answers, and so can you." Postmodernism responds, "I don't have all the answers, and neither do you." If culture is saying "apple" and the church insists on "orange," then big surprise: We're losing ground in society because we're not speaking the same language. In her book *Authentic Parenting in a Postmodern Culture*, Mary DeMuth wrote,

> Evangelicals tend to disdain the culture and the language, preferring the old culture and language. But it's not either/or; it's both/and. We aren't throwing the baby out with the bathwater; we're keeping the baby and changing the bathwater. The gospel remains the same, but the presentation changes.[4]

MISSION POSSIBLE

Along with other seismic shifts we'd undergone, we became convinced that to attract our community to Christ, we had to become missionaries to do it, immersing ourselves in culture as yeast that might ultimately affect the whole batch. We are sent people—missionaries in our neighborhood, our kids' schools, our community, our gym (okay, that was a lie), our favorite restaurants.

The church is no longer central, and therefore people are not drawn to it as they used to be. We couldn't expect anyone to heed us just because we hung a church sign and donned the pastor label. We accepted that the first reaction we should anticipate was skepticism, and the only bridge through that chasm was through *sustained, genuine relationships*. Care of our fellow man, locally and globally, was our best hope to attract people to our Jesus, far more effective than cool music or impersonal mail-outs.

As missionaries have always understood, the key is to study the culture you are passionate about reaching and submerge into that space with respect and love. Our mission field was south Austin, and no church-planting method could be exactly transplanted into our context. We knew we had to do the hard work of cultural immersion, so we put a for-sale sign in our yard and moved to the south side.

Certainly, we could still insist on modernist absolutes, but that approach is not effective for the average postmodern who doesn't know Christ. Neither worldview is all good or all bad, and each has played a significant role in the progression of mankind. However, I spy some gospel standards evident in the postmodern viewpoint that encourage me:

- A sense of global community and care for suffering humanity
- Respect for our earth and its resources
- Authenticity valued over appearance
- A passion for community and honest relationships
- Responsibility and the rejection of consumerism

Not only are these the values of the average postmodern, they completely align with the gospel. We already share common ground, and the best way to connect is to capitalize on it. Church, what if we really loved our neighbors and offered a safe place for community in our homes, *showing* them church rather than just *inviting* them to one? What if we served alongside secular nonprofits rescuing orphans in India? How might the church be perceived if we volunteered with organizations feeding the hungry? What if believers supported environmental groups working toward alternative fuel options? What if we pursued political objectivity, resisting partisan identification that has plagued Western Christianity? Could the very service Jesus required double as evangelism? Have we found a way to become attractive again?

As God explained in Isaiah,

Is not this the kind of fasting I have chosen:
to loose the chains of injustice
    and untie the cords of the yoke,
to set the oppressed free
    and break every yoke? (58:6)

This sounds like the postmodern rejection of individualism for community. Responsibility for each other is the first description of the fast God requires: an abstinence from selfishness, greed, and egotism. Discipleship is not a personal journey with few links to community; it exists for us to spur one another on toward liberation and execute justice for those too trapped to free themselves. It is a lifestyle obsessed with the broken members of our human tribe: those living next to us, in our families, and everywhere someone is devalued. We have a mandate to liberate our fellow man, in every context. We are in this life together; we belong to one another.

This is not about the mechanics of *doing* church. I'm not talking about an infrastructure or strategy. I'm thinking of our core member who brings cakes to her neighbors every week. I'm thinking of our eight families who took in total strangers evacuated from Houston thanks to Hurricane Ike; for a week, our people housed more than eighty evacuees who couldn't afford shelter while the rest of our church brought food and supplies. I'm thinking about two of our men who stood up in court with an abused single mom we met on the streets. I'm thinking of our member who volunteered to organize our downtown cookouts; his business savvy turned that mission into a well-oiled machine of efficiency.

I am here to tell you: the best stuff put out "by ANC" is simply a collection of what our people do in their real lives. There is no substitute for a gathering of missionaries in love with God and their community—no church can reach as far, no organization can be as effective, no mission can burn so hot, no one leader can accomplish as much. I know now more than ever that an organized church is simply a loose structure to hold us together; *people are truly the church*. They are its life and breath and strength. It is you. It is me. The kingdom advances in our small neighborhoods and small acts of love and small moments of faithfulness and small feats of courage. It is not encapsulated in programs and top-down structures but activated through the body of Christ daring to be faithful everywhere we've been planted.

This is not about Brandon and Jen Hatmaker, church planters, because we are ordinary and our church is imperfect, same as yours. This is about the bride of Christ. Church simply provides a nice context for us to live on mission together. It's not about your church and how it is thrilling or failing you. Rather, what kind of bride are *you* helping to prepare? With the glorious addition of you and your gifts, is she becoming radiant? Shane Claiborne wrote, "There is a movement bubbling up that goes beyond cynicism and celebrates a new way of living, a generation that stops complaining about the church it sees and becomes the church it dreams of."[1]

SHARE, PROVIDE, CLOTHE, SHINE

Is [the true fast] not to share your food with the hungry
        and to provide the poor wanderer with shelter—
when you see the naked, to clothe them,
        and not to turn away from your own flesh and
        blood? (Isaiah 58:7)

This is the language of Jesus in Matthew 25, and it attracts postmoderns who are moved not by buildings and events but by compassion and global impact. Mercy to the hungry, poor, homeless, and orphaned has the threefold advantage of administering relief to the most distressed, identifying with Jesus on the deepest level, and drawing the skeptic through an action he is already compelled by.

We've had people join us for social projects who would never join us for a church service. Our deepest cynic served burgers downtown with us six times before she set foot in church; she's a transformed believer now. Leaders of non-profit secular organizations joined our community after our sustained service to their mission. We provided long-term care for a terminal couple with AIDS through Care Communities; after five months they accepted Christ, one month before the husband died. One of our pastors was invited to speak about our mission initiative to all the employees at Walmart after we forged a partnership for our Communities in Schools projects.

Our community work is obviously not unprecedented. We stand on the shoulders of faithful churches that have brought good news for centuries, and we stand beside legions of beautiful faith communities in our generation. My point is that this posture toward a city bears a meaningful witness to the skeptics, nonbelievers, and anti-organized-religion population. What mail-outs, cold invites, media, and strategic marketing are still struggling to do, relationships through justice are accomplishing. It will disappoint the average consumer Christian, but it might be our only hope to convince the lost.

This is more vital than ever because although the postmodern values community and service, that doesn't mean he lives out those values. There is a marked difference between criticizing consumerism and actually resisting consumerism. It is en vogue to broadcast antimaterialism while tweeting via an iPhone upgraded from last year's model. Crying "ecology" is one thing; making environment-friendly choices with our money is another. The average carbon footprint remains high. The marketing world panders to the postmodern rhetoric while selling to us under the table, capitalizing on our duplicity.

The postmodern worldview is challenging to truly live by, not unlike the narrow path we are called to—easy to talk about, hard to actually follow. The church must not only demonstrate its commitment to gospel-based values the postmodern shares but also show her how. Grab her by the hand and work alongside her.

Then your light will break forth like the dawn,
    and your healing will quickly appear;
then your righteousness will go before you,
    and the glory of the LORD will be your rear guard.
Then you will call, and the LORD will answer;
    you will cry for help, and he will say: Here am I.
If you do away with the yoke of oppression,
    with the pointing finger and malicious talk,
and if you spend yourselves in behalf of the hungry
    and satisfy the needs of the oppressed,
then your light will rise in the darkness,
    and your night will become like the noonday.
    (Isaiah 58:8-10)

Clearly, this was our business model. Why waste time on silly finger-pointing when we had such urgent tasks to engage? In one day I spent the morning dealing with malicious talk and the evening working on behalf of the hungry, and there was a clear winner. I was going the way of Isaiah 58, Matthew 25, Luke 22, John 21. These made up the permanent address of light, healing, protection, communion, righteousness, answered prayers. Something broken fused back together, and I was officially off the platform, launched into the adventure.

Believer, your life is too essential to waste on pettiness or word wars, greed or ladder climbing, anger or bitterness, fear or anxiety, regret or disappointment. Life is too short. We must run, not walk, the way of Isaiah 58, embracing authentic faith manifested through mercy and community. Living on mission requires nothing less. It is a grand adventure, a true voyage into the kingdom of God. Would you lose days, months, years pointing fingers and quarreling, or would you rather break yokes of oppression? Imagine what would happen if we all chose the latter.

Our light would rise in the darkness, indeed.

Heavy Influences—Phase Four

- Free Methodist church (www.freemethodistchurch.org)
- *The Tangible Kingdom* by Hugh Halter and Matt Smay
- *unChristian* by David Kinnaman and Gabe Lyons
- *I'm Fine with God . . . It's Christians I Can't Stand* by Bruce Bickel and Stan Jantz

- *Leadership and Self-Deception* by The Arbinger Institute
- *Authentic Parenting in a Postmodern Culture* by Mary E. DeMuth
- Mobile Loaves & Fishes (www.mlf.org)
- The book of Isaiah

Brandon's Take

For the first time in our lives, we weren't trying to create our own opportunities; we were simply trying to respond to the Spirit's leading. That created a very uncomfortable season of waiting. What did we now know? We were being called to something new, faith steps of departure were imminent, and we needed to find out what God was doing in the bigger picture and how we fit into it. How to do this? No idea.

As I look back, I am convinced God was profoundly placing our hearts on kingdom work. Even today that perspective is evident. Not just in *our* lives; it's everywhere. I hear story after story attesting to this kingdom mind-set.

On our journey, God shaped a clear foundation: Kingdom

work, partnership, and focus were central. Although Jesus discussed the kingdom as much as any topic, it's something many believers have no concept of or affection for. Our focus naturally goes to our kingdom, our immediate reality, our goals and passions, and our church.

But that's not what Jesus taught. He told Peter,

> I tell you that you are Peter, and on this rock I will build
> my church, and the gates of Hades will not overcome
> it. I will give you the keys of the kingdom of heaven;
> whatever you bind on earth will be bound in heaven, and
> whatever you loose on earth will be loosed in heaven.
> (Matthew 16:18-19)

Jesus never gave us the keys to His church; He handed over keys to the kingdom. This isn't something to set aside as another symbolic reference. This was Jesus' instruction: place your affections on My kingdom, and *I will build My church*. Bind your heart to things of eternal value, keep your mind on a vision bigger than you, and ensure all your efforts match those affections. Jesus will take care of the rest.

So we began to look for kingdom opportunities. Words cannot do justice to what had gone on before us. The networking, the prayer, the partnership groundwork were already laid out; we had nothing to do with it. It came down to a call from a complete stranger from a mission-minded denomination and culminated in a partnership that spanned across denominations, a city, and a nation just a few days later. We didn't know what it was entirely about (and we are discovering new layers still). We just knew it brought a shift in thinking and, for us, a new way of doing church.

One of our greatest joys is participating in and helping to create partnerships bigger than us. It's not just about Austin New Church; it's about like-minded churches in our city. It's not just about our denominational affiliation; it's cross-denominational. It's not just our own nonprofit efforts; it's partnering with other organizations making a difference.

I've discovered that this journey is not about finding validation as a leader; it's not about our church. It's bigger than that. It's about putting hands and feet to the gospel—our hands and our feet. It's about building bridges with those who won't come to us on Sunday, not as a project but because Jesus loves them and told us to. It's a dangerous journey that requires honesty and vulnerability. It's about the kingdom breaking through in all of our lives. It's about creating a place to belong before people are expected to behave or even believe. If the gospel is good news to all, then it's not just an idea to consider, a time slot on a Sunday, or a task assigned to a select few—it's a life to live. And it's bigger than all of us.

PHASE FIVE: SENT

We see a church where people can find biblical community. We believe that the church should be the best place to build honest and encouraging relationships that speak, share, and seek to live out God's truth.

VALUE:
*Building genuine relationships
with God and each other.*

KEY SCRIPTURE:
1 Corinthians 9:19-23

OUT OF
KINDERGARTEN

I have eaten many lunches with my kids at their elementary school, a heroic endeavor I expect to be rewarded for in heaven. Coincidentally, what weird universe is this where every single elementary school cafeteria has the same smell? Every time I walk in there, I'm transported back to Mulberry Elementary in Houma, Louisiana, 1984. Fun fact: That same year, Principal Babbin had his mouth wired shut after jaw surgery, and we thought we'd merited some sort of divine intervention. Also that year? I played Mrs. Cratchit in our fifth-grade production of *A Christmas Carol* and had to hold Jeremy Doucet's hand during the Christmas dinner prayer; it caused me such mental anxiety that I jacked up my one line ("It's a fine-looking bird, Bob, and we're grateful to have it").

But I digress.

One day, my fourth grader at the time, Gavin, had first lunch, so I sat with him and his fellow preteens for twenty minutes, enjoying deep discussions about gaming systems and online cheats (not as illicit as it sounds). A bonus was watching the girls attempt to get the boys' attention while the guys stuck spaghetti noodles on their lips like mustaches, oblivious. There were a lot of "Dude!" and "That's so gay" comments, after which Gavin glanced at me, silently begging me not to lecture his friends for that slander. Every boy had shaggy soccer hair, styled some awkward ten-year-old way (Gavin swoops his bangs across his forehead with mousse and calls it his "swaive." We don't know where he got this.) They were miniature teenagers—fashion-conscious if not quite girl-conscious, sarcastic, and so electronically sophisticated that their conversation sounded like a foreign language.

Then I watched Caleb's kindergarten class walk in. Every five-year-old had his index finger over his mouth, making the universal "I shall not make excessive noise" sign. Some of the little boys were holding hands. They carried Thomas the Tank Engine and Barbie Fairytopia lunchboxes. Those who spotted a parent started waving like Forrest Gump jumping off the *Jenny* shrimp boat. They unself-consciously wore Disney velcro shoes and outfits that communicated, "I dressed myself." I don't care what anyone says: Kindergarteners are tiny babies. Making them attend the same school as fifth graders should

be illegal. Compared to the preteens, they were so precious
and innocent that I could have burst into tears, risking swift
ridicule from Gavin and his fellow swaive sporters.

My kids' growing-up process is equal parts wonderful and
painful for me. The changes are harder than I thought—and
better than I thought. As much as I treasure the endearment
of early childhood, I'm enjoying my kids' developing maturity in other ways. They might not carry Thomas lunchboxes
or call me Mommy anymore, but sometimes they slip and
call me "Dude," and that has its own charm too.

We quickly grew from the idealistic, innocent "kindergarten" phase of church planting to the grittier, more realistic
"preteen" one. It was no longer the flawless concept tinged
with perfection, but the coarseness had a new charm too.
This phase began by moving our dream out of our heads
and onto the ground (which is about the moment it lost
its imagined "perfection"). And what a grand beginning: a
handful of families meeting in an apartment complex, kids
running helter-skelter, each of us wondering if anyone knew
what they were doing.

There were maybe fifteen of us stumbling through the
messy early stage of vision. We met once a week to pray,
dream, rally. I will forever cherish those who invested at such
an unorganized, chaotic stage. Why they came or stayed can
be attributed only to the call of God on their lives. I'll remain
forever grateful to the core team; they worked their fingers
to the bone with absurd enthusiasm, which propelled us to
keep going.

We were in this thing full time, but everyone else led a normal life. They invested in small pieces, but collectively they lifted the church off the ground. Hospital administrators, teachers, nurses, financial advisers, stay-at-home moms, corporate executives, college kids—a church-planting team is representative of the culture, not a group of paid professionals or full-time ministers. Each partner organized a small corner of ministry, and together it turned into a little baby church.

When it was time to name this thing, we had several options. There were the directional names: Southwest Community, Northeast Fellowship, Westside Family, South Austin blah blah blah. Then there were the hip names: Faith Bridge, Bridgepoint, Crosspoint, Guts Church, Flood Church, Hot Rod Church for Sinners.

We discussed this ad nauseam (not a great time to enact a democracy, church planters), and it emerged. We combed through a year's worth of prayers and journals and correspondence and Bible studies, and we remembered a consistent message:

"We serve *in the new way of the Spirit.*" (Romans 7:6)
"A *new command* I give you: Love one another. As I
   have loved you, so you must love one another."
   (John 13:34)
"Neither circumcision nor uncircumcision means
   anything; what counts is *the new creation.*"
   (Galatians 6:15)
"Pour new wine into *new wineskins.*" (Matthew 9:17)

Thus, Austin New Church was born, giving honor to this new covenant, new way, new love, new life. We've drawn comfort from Jesus' birth in the manger: Humble beginnings (a generous understatement) are a good thing. Relocating from multipurpose rooms to living rooms and back was evidently no cause for alarm; baby Jesus slept in a feeding trough. It was okay that we were disorganized and unrehearsed in explaining why we named our church something so weird. The whole thing felt slippery and intangible and slightly out of control.

It was pretty much the best time of our lives.

In perhaps the finest demonstration of solidarity ever, our best friends moved to Austin from Corpus Christi to start this church with us. Until their house sold, they commuted every weekend, driving back late Sunday night. Instead of the award they deserved for this, they got a laundry list of tasks and a pay cut. Welcome to the glamorous world of church planting. (In *Confessions of a Reformisson Rev.*, the first chapter is titled "Jesus, Our Offering Was $137 and I Want to Use It to Buy Bullets," and that's spot-on.)

Everyone else said, "I'll figure out child care" or "We'll work on finding a location" or "We're putting the feelers out on worship leaders" or "We'll mobilize the prayer team," and before we knew it, a church started emerging out of the chaos. It's not magic; it's hard work by vested people who share a vision for God's kingdom in their city. An influential church is nothing more than a bunch of believers who get in the game and live on mission. This principle holds at fifteen and fifteen thousand people alike.

It was (and still is) all hands on deck. Most hands could give a few hours a week at best, but multiply those hours by fifteen people and add them to the three or four of us working (seemingly) around the clock, and you've got something. If you ever encounter a healthy bride of Christ who gets to act passive and lazy, please call me so I can immediately move my membership there.

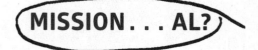

MISSION... AL?

We butchered a lot of terminology back then, knowing what we wanted to become but incapable of describing it unless someone had a minimum of eighty minutes to listen, at which point he'd wave the white flag and retreat, certainly sorry he'd asked. Clearly we wanted to be obedient to the social mandates of Isaiah 58 and Matthew 25, but we also wanted to reach the general south Austin community and lead believers to live on mission in their contexts while also caring for one another. We hoped for some pretty specific fruits:

- Jesus would become supreme—not our church, not us, not a method, not a band, not programs. We

dreamed of a body allegiant far more to Christ than
to ANC.

- ANC would become a disciple factory, rejecting
the language and structures that create spiritually
immature consumers.
- Christ followers would learn to take ownership in
their own spiritual development, not expecting their
church to do all the heavy lifting.
- We would raise awareness of human suffering and
present tangible opportunities to alleviate it.
- Believers, seekers, and skeptics alike could discover
a shift away from the old progression (Believe and
Behave *then* Belong) to something more inviting:
Belong to Believe then Become.[1]
- Weekly community groups would be the life force
of ANC, not weekend attendance. We still have a
great Sunday service. It's simple in presentation and
powerful in worship, but it's a gathering, not the
beginning and end of our faith community.
- ANC would create not only disciples but also
missionaries all over Austin.

This last idea took the longest to develop. While we were
saying "missional," most people thought that meant "mission," and I think we transposed the two for a while as well.
Mission encompassed our work with the homeless community, disadvantaged schools, an orphanage in Mexico, a refor-
estation project in Africa. When we engaged some aspect

of human suffering or care for the earth, it fell under the mission banner.

But even though all our mission work is sustainable and long term, we spend the majority of our lives in our homes, our neighborhoods, at work, in school. It was essential to incorporate the *spirit of mission* into our natural habitats, where the brunt of our influence exists.

Are you a teacher? Your school is a mission field, plain and simple. Business leader, the principles of cultural immersion are absolutely the front door to reaching your colleagues. Stay-at-home mom, the community of mothers raising littles is special—connect with other women intentionally during what can be a lonely and isolating season. Students, you are surrounded by peers hungry for salvation and purpose but deeply cynical about the church; developing language to introduce them to Jesus is noble and urgent. Recovering legalists? First, you are my people. Second, we must replace some entrenched perceptions about culture in order to become missionaries to our neighborhoods. An accurate understanding of grace will wreck the tidy categories we've assigned people and allow us to open our arms wide. Taking Jesus seriously goes well beyond a church service or mission project; He becomes the substance of our whole lives.

Missional at its core means "sent." It is the opposite of "come to us." So many believers have selected their pet concept of the Great Commission—they read, "*Make disciples* of all nations," but neglect the prerequisite instruction: "*Go.*" Going is the noble history of the Trinity. God sent

Jesus to dwell among fallen humanity—not to visit, not to remain separated, not to detach, but to immerse. He was the supreme Missionary to mankind, submerged in culture, among the people He wanted to rescue. Upon Jesus' resurrection, God sent the Spirit from the heights of heaven to the heart of every believer, an indwelling.

Among, beside, within—this is the way of the Trinity. God has gone to people since the day He walked in the garden. People came to Him only *after* an encounter, *after* a revelation, *after* belief. He is the initiator, meeting humans on their turf in the middle of their chaos. God understood that we were too broken and confused to find Him in His divine dwelling places. Once we belong to Him, we know where to look for sweet communion, but until then, He comes to us.

God sent Jesus; Jesus sent the Spirit; and together they send us as ambassadors for the gospel, immersed in humanity and living in the harvest field. On a practical level, why would we expect unbelievers to come to church with no provocation? What do they know of the beauty of the Spirit? Why would they be attracted to an unknown Savior or a community that feels like worshipping Him? Certainly the dechurched and rechurched with a context for God might be attracted through familiar venues. But why would cynics join a weekend celebration of a God they don't know, especially One who has been so poorly represented by His people?

The message must be brought to them, in their individual contexts, where they are and how they are. This, in fact, is the mission of the church. In *Breaking the Missional Code,* Ed Stetzer and David Putman wrote,

> The church is one of the few organizations in
> the world that does not exist for the benefit of its
> members. The church exists because God, in his
> infinite wisdom and infinite mercy, chose the church
> as his instrument to make known his manifold
> wisdom in the world.[2]

I used to reside exclusively in Christian subculture: I read James Dobson to learn how to parent, studied Dave Ramsey to learn how to budget, sang Third Day for inspiration, went to Women of Faith conferences for encouragement, consulted Christian Coalition voting guides to see how to vote, and read Tim LaHaye for my fiction fix. This was the controlled bubble I lived in with a few hundred of my closest friends. Stetzer and Putman wrote,

> Some call this the "herding effect." When you
> are running in the middle of a herd of buffalo,
> everything looks identical. What we see becomes
> our reality. We think that everyone around us knows
> where we are, and they can come to the church if
> they want to be like us.[3]

It's not that Christian influence is bad (well, it's not all bad), but if followed exclusively, it distorts our perception of real life and our role in it. We turn a blind eye to the customs, cultures, communities, and contexts where people live their lives with different preferences and worldviews right next door to us. The problem with Christian segregation is that God asked us to be on mission with Him, sent us to some group of people somewhere, and wants us to minister to them in a way that meets their needs by speaking their language.

This is a sticking point with a lot of believers. I worry the Christian community has accepted an insidious shift from laboring for others to prioritizing our own rights. We've perpetuated a group identity as misunderstood and persecuted, defending our positions and preferring to be right over being good news. We've bought the lie that connecting with people on their terms is somehow compromising, that our refusal to proclaim our moral ground from word one is a slippery slope. It has become more vital to protect our own station than advocate for a world that needs Jesus, who came to us, wrapped in our skin, speaking our language. If we were not too beneath Christ, who died for us while we were still sinners, then how dare we take a superior position over any other human being? How lovely is a faith community that goes forth as loving sisters and brothers rather than angry defenders and separatists.

OFFERING A TANGIBLE KINGDOM

As we began dreaming about how Austin New Church would be expressed in our community, viewpoints like this from Halter and Smay started messing with us:

> Church must not be the goal of the gospel anymore.
> Church should not be the focus of our efforts or
> the banner we hold up to explain what we're about.
> Church should be what ends up happening as a
> natural response to people wanting to follow us, be
> with us, and be like us as we are following the way
> of Christ.[1]

This is certainly consistent with postmodern society, but how does it work? We've relied on the church to represent Jesus for so long; taking on that job ourselves leaves something of a vacuum. If the church staff isn't responsible for transformative change in everyone's life, how else will it happen?

Sunday attendance is often the bull's-eye, but that inherently creates a flawed system. When the final goal is church, some unhealthy expectations are attached. The pastor becomes central, and too much hinges on his personality, his teaching, his life. Facing pressure without and within, pastors learn to exhibit an ideal caricature of their real self and forfeit authenticity for image. This has a trickle-down effect on the congregation, and honest community struggles to emerge.

And don't get me started on how much pressure is then put on the sermon. It becomes everyone's best hope to convince the skeptics in our midst, which it sometimes can but often can't. How many sermons have actually altered your life? One thirty-minute message a week is rarely the catalyst for transformation.

Paul understood what drew people to faith: "But we were gentle among you, like a nursing mother taking care of her own children. So, being affectionately desirous of you, we were ready to share with you not only the gospel of God but also our own selves, because you had become very dear to us" (1 Thessalonians 2:7-8, ESV).

Sermon-centered evangelism leaves too much work to the paid pros and omits a meaningful relational context. Halter and Smay wrote,

When we focus on the message only, what are we saying to people? Maybe that they really aren't dear to us? Is it possible that to share four great truths about God without giving the listeners a part of our lives might communicate the wrong thing? Paul knew that a message without an attractive tangible person embodying and delivering it would fall on deaf ears or be lost amid all the other faiths of that time. What makes the gospel good news isn't the concept, but the real-life person who has been changed by it.[2]

How much more tangible is the gospel when someone experiences it over weeks and months with a real believer whom he or she can ask questions of and learn from by observation? When a Christian consistently treats someone with compassion or demonstrates integrity at work, the gospel wins a hearing. We can continue to invite unbelievers to church, but we must first invite them into our lives. Have them over, go to dinner, welcome them in. Create a safe place for them to belong without agenda; they needn't worry about following our Christian rules yet (or pretending to in front of us). We must become their advocates, embracing them as dear friends so they might one day feel comfortable belonging with us. This is not a strategy for rapid church growth, but the patient hard work of love is the way of Christ. It is the subversive path into the kingdom.

The spirit of mission means that we serve our neighbors

long before they are brothers or sisters in Christ. Putting their needs first, we sacrifice to love them. We act on their behalf, not with condescension as Christians Who Have All the Answers but as their true friends. We can skip judging them; that's not our job. Either God can sanctify or He can't. We needn't yank the work of transformation out of His hands, for the love. It isn't our responsibility to defend our values and prioritize our message over our posture. We inherited a kingdom that cannot be shaken; we are an unthreatened people. God will stay on His throne without our rigorous defense. Halter and Smay wrote,

> Jesus didn't, and we shouldn't. He doesn't need us to stick up for him; he needs us to represent him, to be like him, to look like him and to talk like him, to be with people that he would be with, and to take the side of the "ignorant" instead of those in the "know."[3]

Love has won infinitely more converts than theology. The first believers were drawn to Christ's mercy long before they understood His divinity. That brings us back to the over-emphasis on Sunday morning as the front door: If love is the most effective way—and the Bible says it is—then how much genuine love can one pastor show an entire congregation? His bandwidth is not wide enough; this is a crippling, impossible burden. When he fails to connect with every person (which he will), the congregation becomes disgruntled because he can't fulfill what should have been their mission. Nor can a random group of strangers standing in a church lobby offer legitimate community to some sojourner who walks in the door.

Believer, your pastor or your church can never reach your coworker like you can. They do not have the sway over your neighbor who has been entrusted to you. No one better than you can love your wayward brother. One decent sermon cannot influence a disoriented person in the same way your consistent presence in her life can. While organized religion provokes mostly skepticism for the average postmodern, a genuine relationship with a Christ follower on mission can reframe the kingdom, making a fresh perception possible. Then that person discovers that church is not a place you go—it's a people you belong with. The building is simply the place where you celebrate God together.

RIGHT TO
REMAIN SILENT

Paul addressed the missional lifestyle with a better explanation than any I've ever heard: "Though I am free and belong to no one, I have made myself a slave to everyone, to win as many as possible" (1 Corinthians 9:19).

This statement contains so much depth that we could unpack it for weeks. The term *free* involves more theological layers than we can address here, but in a literal sense, a free person serves no other man. That is the basic meaning of *free*. He is not owned; he doesn't have to defer to another; he has rights and privileges because of his position. In fact, within the first-century context, a free man likely had servants to meet *his* needs—certainly not the other way around.

This is the elevated station we are awarded at salvation; we no longer serve the rigorous demands of the law. We are not bound by its restraints or confined by its limitations. We serve in a new way of the Spirit, which overpowers the letter of the law. We are granted a new set of rights:

- We have the right to be called children of God, with the privileges that entails.[1]
- We have the full rights of children of God: We have His Spirit within, and we are heirs to the kingdom.[2]
- We have the right to eat from the tree of life and enter heaven's gates.[3]
- We have the right to sit with Jesus on His throne one day.[4]
- We are free from the stranglehold of guilt and sin.[5]
- We are free from legalistic human commands and teachings.[6]

By our adoption into the family of God, we become royalty. We have every privilege and right the King grants His children. We are free from conventional boundaries and enjoy exemptions because of our rank. It is within our entitlement to apply our advantages and live as the heirs we are.

This is all courtesy of Jesus, who forfeited His rights so we could have them instead.

When we assume the posture of a slave to all, we adopt the voluntary humility of Christ, who surrendered His rights for the salvation of mankind. The literal implication of slave

means we behave "as a real slave"—labor as one, defer to
those we serve, are diligent to please and not offend, and act
as if we have no privileges at all—to win as many as possible.

Eighteenth-century theologian Matthew Henry wrote,

> A heart warmed with zeal for God, and breathing
> after the salvation of men, will not plead and insist
> upon rights and privileges in bar to this design.
> Those manifestly abuse their power in the gospel
> who employ it not to edification but destruction,
> and therefore breathe nothing of its spirit.[7]

As we engage a broken world, standing stubbornly on
principle or privilege indicates an immature heart that prefers to be right rather than seek the redemption of his neighbor. When we lead with doctrine before love, we brutalize
the spirit of the doctrine we're prioritizing. Insisting that
unbelievers or disoriented believers defer to our convictions
is the quickest way to repel them from God. Even if our
posture isn't arrogant, broadcasting our extreme Christian
principles without sensitivity makes us seem so weird that
we'll lose credibility anyway. (An extremely conservative
believer said in the company of our non-Christian friends,
"We believe Halloween costumes are pagan," and it was
like throwing an Awkward Grenade into the conversation,
which—big shock—was abandoned about six seconds later
so everyone could return to their pagan homes. I just can't
even.) We're leading with the wrong foot, and we might

never get a chance to correct that offense. Theology very naturally follows belief, but belief very rarely follows judgment.

Paul presented the most superior posture we can assume: "I am your slave." What if your neighbor came to understand that you wanted to be his servant? How would my colleague soften to the gospel if I set my agenda aside and became her constant slave? How would our communities be transformed if our churches became servants to our cities? If at every turn believers labored for others as if they were our masters, we could not be ignored for long.

This position has driven ANC since its conception. As we moved toward the official launch of our church, we reimagined its public birth scheduled for Easter 2008, exactly one year after our profound experience the Easter before. We could have revealed our church to the south Austin community via bullhorns and billboards, but that wasn't consistent with our mission. As slaves to our city, our first Sunday service was a massive food drive benefiting the Capital Area Food Bank; it encompassed twenty neighborhoods, and we collected more than one ton of food. The message we wanted to communicate was: "Nice to meet you, south Austin. Austin New Church is here to be your servant."

We came to *their* neighborhoods, to *their* homes, to *their* communities. We couldn't expect anyone to come to us without some reason. (In a hilarious twist, two of the three local network affiliates picked up the project as their Easter segment on the evening news. One network presented a lovely piece on the hundred of us—about seventy people connected with ANC and thirty unaffiliated who just liked the idea—schlepping boxes of food, and the other network dropped us for a story called "Pooches on Parade" about yippy little dogs dressed in drag and working a runway. True story. This is the yin and yang we've come to expect in church planting.)

We were on the ground, dying to get past the launch so we could concentrate on being a church rather than starting a church.

With relief, we moved beyond the first service in rented space, where attendance was totally inflated with well-wishers and the mildly curious. While our core team looked around in disbelief, we kept saying, "They're not all staying. Don't get too excited."

Lofty expectations are the worst enemy of a church planter. Do not imagine that Austin New Church is some fast-growing, hard-charging headliner; the number of people we have a few years in is so insignificant in this city of a million-plus that it's not even worth mentioning. Nor has church planting been a magical journey of rainbows and unicorns. (I'm envisioning Brandon in my daughter's room an hour before that first church gathering, cutting "bulletins" with her scrapbook paper cutter.)

Then there was the day Tray, our associate pastor, sent a test e-mail through our new database system, thinking it would go only to his inbox; instead, it went to every single recipient. The first corporate message from ANC was: "This is a test e-mail. Blah, blah, blah . . . your mom." I'm pretty sure insulting people's mothers is far from an excellent church-growth strategy, and this was the first in a long list of blunders and missteps.

BREAKING
THE CODE

In addition to our own capacity for self-destruction, we faced an uphill battle. Not only is Austin extremely unchurched and resistant to the gospel, but we discovered that south Austin adorably is called "the church planter's graveyard." The concept of missional church involves understanding a culture and developing language and structures to most effectively reach it for Christ—in other words, starting with them, not us. Breaking the code is particularly difficult in south Austin. Countless church start-ups haven't made it here.

No one model will fit every context. A church positioned to reach empty nesters in a retirement community in Florida is going to operate much differently from one sent to minister to young adult urbanites in Seattle. Dropping a church anywhere based on our preferences without considering those of the community is a recipe for failure. It is not on mission to say, "This is the way we've always liked it. Take it or leave it." That is being the master, not the slave.

Our challenge in the church planter's graveyard is that there is no one demographic here. For other parts of Austin, you can summarize the people groups with some accuracy: young white families, second-generation Hispanics, affluent professionals, low-income black families. But in south Austin, the demographic pie chart has a lot of slivers. Roughly 60 percent of the kids attending the school where we meet are from single-parent families: 65 percent Hispanic, 15 percent black, 15 percent white, and 5 percent Asian. The Hispanic tribe is divided between first-generation Mexican natives and second-generation Hispanics in the small-business realm who are entering middle class. Then there are dual-income white families moving in, and two or three pricier 'hoods thrown in for good measure. Some neighborhoods have existed for fifty years, but an influx of new developments draws a totally different crowd. South Austin is racially, socioeconomically, and culturally diverse.

We could have stood on principle and organized our church however we liked, but since we were serious about reaching people who actually lived in south Austin, we had to study the nuances of the culture: How do they think? What are their values? What events have shaped their histories? What are their goals? Starting with demographic segmentations is okay, but a slave must learn the finer distinctives of his master if he is going to serve effectively. We must be prepared not just to meet Mrs. Hispanic Matriarch or Mr. Upwardly Mobile White Graduate with 2.3 Kids but to discover who they are beneath their oversimplified categories.

For example, with a high percentage of Hispanics in south Austin, we know most grew up connected to the Catholic Church. Whether or not they are committed patrons, that is their familiar culture. So we include a few liturgical elements in our service: weekly Communion similar to the Catholic method of coming forward, prayer candles, a corporate recitation of the Lord's Prayer, and a spoken blessing over the people at the close of each service. There are plenty of potential elements that honor Christ; we've simply chosen a few that also provide a familiar context to our community.

Again, this isn't just about church planting. This principle affects all Christ followers who want to live on mission. Our most attractive offering is a genuine relationship, so we must resist quick assumptions and settle into longevity with people. If you were attempting to understand me, you could study a fact grouping but would draw incomplete conclusions. Here's one set: I grew up in a lower-middle-class, blue-collar town in Kansas; I joined the party sorority in college; I ride on the back of my husband's Harley; and I have tattoos.

If that were the end of your Jen Hatmaker research, you would see only part of the picture. Those facts are all true, but they don't define me exclusively. You might assume I was a rebellious party type with shallow spiritual history (I might be a little rebellious). Making quick assumptions is premature; there is always more than the obvious traits we first see. We do others a disservice by summarizing their lives on superficial or categorical observations. Case in point—here is a second fact grouping about me: I am a pastor's daughter, a pastor's wife, and a Christian author; and I graduated magna cum laude from a conservative Baptist college. Again, you might expect certain behaviors or preferences based on this litany, but you'd be surprised. If this was your only input, then meeting me in person would be confusing. (I wore a Run-D.M.C. T-shirt and weird hat to church last night, and a friend introduced me to her coworker by saying, "*This* is our senior pastor's wife. See what I'm saying about our church?" Whatever the opposite of the senior pastor's wife stereotype is, that's me.)

One twenty-five-year-old college graduate might live on your block because his family is dysfunctional and he moved as far away as possible. Another twenty-five-year-old college graduate might live there because his beloved parents are one neighborhood over in the house he grew up in. Believers, this is why we have to do the hard work of missional living. We cannot possibly know all there is to know about anyone without digging deep, getting close, and providing a safe place for people to be known.

This takes the one investment that comprises our hottest commodity: time. We invite people in again and again and again, peeling back layers and slowly discovering that God has surrounded us with beautiful people whom He loves. There is no time limit, no statute of limitations. Sharing our lives with dear people to win them to Jesus is the substance of Christianity, the delightful work we've been commissioned to.

CHANGELINGS

Paul expounded on living missionally: "To the Jews I became like a Jew, to win the Jews. To those under the law I became like one under the law (though I myself am not under the law), so as to win those under the law" (1 Corinthians 9:20).

If I'm honest, I'll admit this part of missional living is much harder for me than engaging the most hostile skeptic. Because I lived under the fear of the law for so long, I am overly sympathetic to disoriented sojourners and unfairly impatient with conservative evangelicals. My tolerance for silly rules and fear-based legalism is low, and I struggle with a very unmissional response to believers who lean toward the law. This is immature and un-Christlike, and all I can say is I'm working on it.

I want the wisdom of Paul, who wasn't compelled to lecture on Christian freedom and its liberties but respected other believers' convictions and joined their rituals. It was more important to win them to Jesus' mercy than to demonstrate his understanding of Jesus' freedom. Their legal restraints were love restraints for Paul, and his message was unpolluted by offensiveness.

Commentator Albert Barnes said this of kingdom behavior: "How worthy of religion! How elevated the conduct! . . . No man would do this who had not a greatness of intellect that would rise above narrow prejudices; and who had not a nobleness of heart that would seek at personal sacrifice the happiness of all men."[1]

If we're going to win people, then let's win people. We do whatever it takes—within the boundaries of law and neutral practices without moral significance—to attract people to the glorious mercy of Jesus. When love regulates our liberty, we create a context to share the gospel and have it actually received. If people are offended by God Himself, by His authority, His Word, His Son, His history, there is less we can do about that. They will ultimately have to wrestle with Him. But if they are offended by our representation of God, then we'll answer for our arrogance. We can help that, and we had better do it.

We should not stubbornly stand on principle at any point along the belief spectrum. Whether persuading a legalist to grace or an atheist to faith, it is our high calling to innocently conform to their worldview in any possible way to earn a hearing for the gospel. Jesus ate with sinners, created wine for partygoers, fished with fishermen, held the children of mothers, taught in the temple with teachers, worshipped in synagogues with the faithful. All things to all people, not bound by convention, public opinion, appearance, legalism, or even His own rights.

Paul went on, "To those not having the law I became like one not having the law (though I am not free from God's law but am under Christ's law), so as to win those not having the law. To the weak I became weak, to win the weak" (1 Corinthians 9:21-22).

Maybe it's my tattoos talking, but this is my favorite missional mandate. Because the perception of Christians as self-righteous segregationists is so prevailing, it is such a pleasure to represent a new expression of faith. For me this is not hard, this is not work, this is not a sacrifice, this is not uncomfortable. A missional approach to a disoriented world has made discipleship fun again. To put it into highly intelligent terms, I get to skip all the church-speak and level with people authentically. I can accept a lovely glass of red wine at a neighbor's house and later get an earful about her marriage struggles. Brandon organizes neighborhood Texas Hold 'em nights to show those men another face of the pastorate; consequently, he's the first person they call in crisis. The eight families in our community group throw Halloween bashes and Christmas extravaganzas and potluck dinners and pool parties in our little subdivision. It's the smallest corner of the world, but it's the one we've been sent to, and we consider ourselves missionaries here.

We have groups all over south Austin, permeating their neighborhoods with joy, love, and the spirit of Jesus. The members of our young-marrieds group, who don't even have their own kids yet, throw birthday parties once a month for children with a parent in prison. One group invited women from their neighborhood to form a Race for the Cure team, and they ran the 5K together. (Jesus was serious about caring for sick people, so we should be too—I don't know anyone who hasn't been affected by cancer.) Another group meets once a week at a local school and landscapes for free.

We have a newlywed couple who are fluent in Spanish; they are both Hispanic, and she is a Mexican native. They were so driven to impact their culture for Christ that ANC rented them a house on the east side (entirely Spanish speaking and low income). We could never reach that community the way they do. Intentionally planted there, they invite neighbors into their home for dinners and parties; they hang out with the students who attend the elementary school across the street. They organize neighborhood cleanups and work with the school administration. They both have real jobs; this is just their life. They don't "do missions"; they are missionaries living in their own personal harvest field.

Outside of organized events, we all deliberately invite people into our homes—nothing revolutionary, just dinner, laughing, connecting. Willing to redefine "what counts," we joyfully legitimize the hours spent investing in people. These moments are no less valid than two hours a week at an organized Bible study. In fact, if our people are living on mission in their own lives, I cannot imagine anything more affirming. This is how ANC prioritizes relational community as the central means of mission, evangelism, and ultimately transformation.

Brandon's Take

God had clearly shifted our thinking and changed the trajectory of our lives. He put us in a place where blind faith was replaced with either obedience or blatant disobedience. We had to choose one or the other. It was that obvious. We searched out how God was already developing this vision. It didn't just come from a book I read or a lecture I heard; it was coming from deep inside, a very spiritual stirring. We saw it throughout our city. It was developing through conversations with other pastors in our city. It emerged through discussions with other church planters seeking to contextualize the gospel through incarnational community. I had a desire to experience the Spirit at levels I hadn't encountered. It was surfacing through my transformed heart and the unexpected fullness Jen and I experienced when we moved outside our comfort zone as leaders and followers.

I noticed a pattern. I was feeling something my spirit had been craving, something that had been missing. For my entire Christian journey, I've felt one click away from full, one click away from true joy, one click away from contentment. Reluctant to admit it, I had a constant desire for more, a nagging hope to be "fed" beyond what I was experiencing.

You're a pastor. How could that be? I'd heard these words all my life from people "wanting to go deeper." I'd heard it way too much, and it seemed selfish. They'd jump from church to church, hoping the void would be filled. Many are now looking outside the church.

As a pastor, I'm instantly threatened by these comments. My nature is to take a defensive posture, dig in my heels, and consider their words an indictment on my teaching ability. However, I no longer think it's the sole result of poor teaching. I believe it's an indictment on our focus: We're trying to fill the void with something that will never be sufficient. There will never be enough knowledge to fill the cracks of Christian maturity without the fruit of selfless service manifested in our lives. Our lives must reflect this heart of Christ, or we will always remain one click away.

Scripture talks clearly about fullness that is found only in love. Paul said to the Ephesians, "I pray that you, being rooted and established in love, may have power, together with all the Lord's holy people, to grasp how wide and long and high and deep is the love of Christ, and to *know this love that surpasses knowledge*—that you may be *filled to the measure* of all the fullness of God" (3:17-19, emphasis added).

If we've been in church for years yet aren't full, are we really hungry for more knowledge? In our busy lives, do we really need another program or event? Do we really need to be fed more of the Word, or are we simply undernourished from an absence of living the Word? Maybe we love God, but are we loving others? If our faith is about us, then we are not just hungry—our spirits are starving.

The result? We church hop or never go because they're not providing enough. Maybe we spend too much attention on ourselves instead of becoming a people on mission. In Ephesians 4, Paul wrote that if we prepare ourselves for "works of service," we will become mature, complete, perfected, and not lacking in anything (verse 12; James 1:4). Isn't that what we're looking for? It's hard to grasp; it's a paradox—but those who've experienced it can testify to it.

In John 13, Jesus washed the disciples' feet, an act even Jewish servants were not required to do. He closed this physical parable with these words: "I have set you an example that you should do as I have done for you. Very truly I tell you, no servant is greater than his master, nor is a messenger greater than the one who sent him. Now that you know these things, you will be blessed if you do them" (verses 15-17).

IN THE CITY,
FOR THE CITY

Obviously, geographic small groups are not new, but their purpose has often been limited by exclusivity: "This is *our* group for us to do life together." "Our six families have been together for four years." As small-group pastor for years, Brandon observed that community groups structured mainly for the benefit of their members have about a three-year shelf life. At that point, the ties dissolve or the fellowship wanes, and they usually disband.

I believe more than simply losing interest, small groups like this evaporate because they aren't on mission, and frankly, that gets boring and unfulfilling. How long can we sit in the same living room or Sunday school class with the same people talking about the same stuff? How many discussions can we have about Sunday's sermon? How long can we sacrifice a night a week for a basic repeat of the last gathering? It runs out because we weren't created to serve ourselves; we're not wired to take the role of master, but slave. Blessing blessed people eventually leaves us empty, and despite a church system designed to meet *our* needs, these words come out of our mouths: "I'm not being fed."

I believe the largest factor in feeling unfed is not feeding others. It has less to do with your pastor's preaching style or the curriculum you're studying. We have an innate craving to live on mission with God in the dangerous, exciting world. Out there is where we come to life, get over ourselves, are fed. Fulfillment exists in becoming a slave to everyone in order to win someone to Jesus. Discipleship was never simply about learning; it was constructed on *living*.

Honestly, the last thing we need is another sermon. I couldn't count the sermons I've heard, yet almost none of my transformational moments took place in a church pew. Are you kidding me? I've been a believer for thirty-four years—pastor's daughter, Baptist college student, pastor's wife, Bible teacher, Christian author, church/camp/conference/revival enthusiast, Christian poster child. I thought I was well beyond transformation. A little refining? Sanding some rough edges? Sure. But transformation? I don't mean to be condescending, and by that I mean talking down to you, but you must not know me and my track record.

When what to my pious eyes should appear? *Transformation*

that interrupted my entire life. Not in the form of a brilliant teacher showing me the original language treasures of the Word. Not in the form of another Bible study that finally cured my spiritual glitches. Not through writing another book or reading someone else's. Not from speaking at women's conferences and meeting exceptional believers all over the country. Not from a single second spent on a church campus.

Transformation came in the form of dirty homeless men and abandoned kids. It came through abused women and foster children. It came through neighbors crying at my kitchen table. Transformation began with humility, even humiliation. It started with conviction and discipline. It increased through loss, not gain. It grew through global exposure and uncomfortable questions. It was born out of rejection, replanted in new soil. It was not found in my Christian subculture but in the eyes of my neighbors, the needs of my city, the cries of the nations. It was through subtraction, not addition, that transformation engulfed me, and I'll tell you something:

I am not the same.

ANC is a missional church not only because that position reaches this world but because that approach makes true disciples. If an endless array of Bible studies, programs, church events, and sermons have left you dry, please hear this: *living on mission where you've been sent* will transform your faith journey. At the risk of oversimplifying it, I've seen missional living cure apathy better than any sermon, promote healing quicker than counseling, deepen discipleship more than Bible studies, and create converts more effectively than events.

It transforms both the master and the slave.

Our community groups meet two weeks a month for traditional fellowship and discussion (this is deliberately inclusive and the front door into our church family); they meet one week for mission work with our nonprofit partners in the city; and they spend the last week apart to intentionally live on mission: inviting neighbors over for dinner, going out for coffee with a coworker, hosting poker night at the Hatmakers.

Instead of the decidedly weird labels of "mission" and "missional" work, we call the whole effort: Love Your Neighbor, Serve Your City. Because this is the priority, we help fund our community groups' projects, which they have complete autonomy over. They have permission and freedom to reach their neighbors the best way they know how. Halloween barbecue for your street? Paid for. Extreme Room Makeover for the after-school care room at your partner school? Covered. Rather than spend our budget on impersonal marketing that will probably draw seven people, we put it in the hands of our missionaries, who are actually reaching real people for Jesus. It just makes sense.

Before we established this structure, a young believer told us, "I really want to do this stuff, but I just don't know how." That is exactly why we gave organization to a lifestyle that is better lived organically. Our hope is that by joining hands and learning to live on mission collectively, serving together will work its transformative magic and *become* organic, the most natural thing in the world.

Mission feeds itself; it is terrifically self-propelling. One member intentionally walked with her neighbor every morning for months and then received an e-mail from her that said: "I don't quite understand what motivates you, but can I join your community group?" Bam. After months of conversations in his driveway, one man asked a church member to discuss his doubts about the cult he was raised in. Another unaffiliated family volunteered with a community group for the Livestrong challenge, and they showed up at church the next Sunday. After a group renovated a classroom for a deserving teacher, she joined their community.

This is a good time to mention that not everyone we touch turns to gold, or to Jesus. They are not all automatically or quickly drawn to faith or church or even our community groups. We've not discovered the first-ever 100 percent effective evangelism strategy. It's slow, cumbersome. Compared to more aggressive tactics, we sometimes wonder if this is working. This doesn't target believers who might simply have a church affair with us; it involves the patient work of introducing people to Jesus for the first time, and that is notoriously slower than convincing other Christians to jump ship. Plus, it can be awkward and clunky, and we are human people who don't always feel magically transformed because we are loving folks with intention. Sometimes we just feel cranky.

It's too early to make definitive statements about this approach; we've been at it for only a few years. Reaching out at least as much as we reach in is not a spiritual magic bullet;

grace is. There is no fix-all outside of the miraculous work Jesus already did on the cross. We don't earn increased favor or cure Christian apathy or solve all the social ills or create some ideal church. Serving people is not heaven's requirement, only a response to heaven's mercy.

Have we seen marginalized and jaded people come to faith or at least take steps closer? Yes. Are the numbers enough to cause shock and awe? No, but since our launch, more than 50 percent of our growth is from new believers, the first person we baptized was homeless when we met her, and more than 80 percent of our adults are connected in missional community groups. It feels right. It feels honest and relational and true. It makes sense to introduce people to Jesus in their natural habitat, where they can meet Him in real life, where He does His best work. It's sort of organic, which often feels unstructured and loose—but maybe that's my formal evangelical training talking, which tends to rebel against loving people first before whacking them over the head with my doctrine.

There is no formula to living on mission. What works in my middle-class neighborhood in south Austin might be the weirdest thing in the world for your affluent urban community. There is no such thing as "Week One—invite neighbor to dinner, Week Two—organize a book club with work friends, Week Three—work with a nonprofit, Week Four— serve the poor. This is the winning schedule." Those tactics might be wildly successful in one place and fall flat in another. Formulas tend to fixate on the details and accidentally miss the point, so don't transplant our vision into your context without breaking the code for your specific culture. There is no magic to living on mission either. Speak the language of the people you're sent to; that's pretty much it. When you can, conform innocently, value what they value, enjoy what they enjoy, go where they might go, think as they might think. Connect with them on their terms, not yours. If you live around intellectuals, that's your avenue; the Bible should keep them occupied for the rest of their lives. If you live in a creative community, connect through the arts; they'll ultimately discover the beauty of God to be overwhelming. If music, then music. If sports, then sports. Be it books, movies, conversation, exercise, hunting, parenting, social work, community activism, camping, coffee, good food, good wine, or any good thing—decode the love language of the tribe around you, and speak it. It's not rocket science. Win them over to you, and you'll have the best chance to win them over to Christ.

Paul said, "I have become all things to all people so that by all possible means I might save some. I do all this for the sake of the gospel, that I may share in its blessings" (1 Corinthians 9:22-23).

Don't imagine that living on mission means we connect with culture by leaving Jesus out of the equation. Nothing could be further from the truth. God's kingdom reigning in the lives of our neighbors is our supreme motivation. We do all this for the sake of the gospel. Living on mission immersed in culture as its slave simply primes the pump. It creates a meaningful context to ultimately introduce people to Christ, the reason we live and breathe. When I think about the gracious, transformative work of Jesus reaching the people I live by and love, I lose my breath. I want this goodness for them so badly. Nothing is better than Jesus. He is truly better than life.

Sometimes the pump doesn't need to be primed. On a monthly girls' night out with the women from our neighborhood, my friend Jenny sat by a new neighbor who pestered her half to death about why she had moved to Austin (to start ANC), and when Jenny finally explained it, sort of, this lady whipped out her BlackBerry and asked for directions: "I'm coming on Sunday. We've been dying to get back into a church." No priming necessary. You'll know which is which. In our community, people are hungry to have a meaningful spiritual discussion; they just don't want to have it with a Christian weirdo who doesn't even know their last name.

I'm sharing in the blessings of the gospel more than I have in my entire life. Not just church, but my life in Jesus for His kingdom has become the most fun, fulfilling venture of my Christian experience. I am so confident in the gospel and its effect on humanity. The baby is so compelling, and if changing the bathwater introduces more people to Him, then sign me up.

It's fitting that *slave* is from a group of words meaning "bonded," which is the same root word used in Titus 2:3 about women "addicted to much wine." In other words, as slaves to our neighbors, our cities, the people of the nations, we are addicted to them. We cannot get enough of them in our homes, in our lives. The more we love them, the more we want to love them. We are addicts for mission, bonded to people for the dream of the gospel in their lives.

This is the mission we are all called to as believers, the noble task of the church. It's not enough to be theologically brilliant without the heart of a missionary. It's sometimes intangible work planted in the messy soil of relationships instead of the cleaner territory of theology. It is slow, often maddening. It requires the patience of Job and the maturity of Paul to execute the mission of Jesus. Living on mission will be misinterpreted and criticized—count on it. Cultural immersion is basically a commitment to being misunderstood.

Amid the fabric of community and developing relationships, you'll often wonder if this is doing anything for the kingdom, but when your neighbor in crisis rings your doorbell at one in the morning, you'll remember that it is. You'll be more convinced when they are drawn to the beauty of Jesus after witnessing His kingdom consistently breaking through in your life. Perhaps even more so when their children are baptized. Weeks, months, years—we are bonded to people as long as it takes. The battle is for the souls of humanity, and our secret weapon is love. The King and His kingdom will reign supreme—that is settled. The only question is: Will you help contend for it?

Dr. Martin Luther King Jr. said it best at a Prayer Pilgrimage for Freedom in 1957:

When the history books are written in the future, the historians will have to look back and say, "There lived a great people . . . a people who injected *new meaning* into the veins of civilization . . . a people that gave *new integrity* and a *new dimension of love* to our civilization." When that happens, the morning stars will sing together, and the sons of God will shout for joy.[1]

It's the "new" the whole world is waiting for.

Heavy Influences—Phase Five

- *Planting Missional Churches* by Ed Stetzer
- *Breaking the Missional Code* by Ed Stetzer and David Putman
- *Confessions of a Reformission Rev.* by Mark Driscoll
- *Organic Church* by Neil Cole
- Austin New Church Core Team
- *A Call to Conscience: The Landmark Speeches of Dr. Martin Luther King, Jr.*, edited by Clayborne Carson and Kris Shepard
- Austin Church Planters Network

Notes

FOREWORD
1. *A Perfect World*, directed by Clint Eastwood (Burbank, CA: Warner Bros., 1993).
2. Rick Meigs, Friend of Missional, www.friendofmissional.org (accessed March 18, 2014).

PHASE ONE: BREAKING DOWN
READER, BEWARE: LIFE-ALTERING PRAYER AHEAD
1. Delirious?, "Rain Down," *World Service* © 2002 Furious? Records.
2. Shane Claiborne, *The Irresistible Revolution* (Grand Rapids, MI: Zondervan, 2006), 39.

JAMES, JESUS, AMOS, AND THEM
1. Martin Luther King Jr., quoted in Clayborne Carson and Kris Shepard, eds., *A Call to Conscience* (New York: Warner Books, 2001), 213–214.

WARNING: THE PROBLEMS ARE BAD
1. Jeffrey D. Sachs, *The End of Poverty* (New York: Penguin Books, 2005), 18.
2. Sachs, *The End of Poverty*, 18–19.
3. http://www.callandresponse.com/about.html (link discontinued).
4. Anup Shah, "Poverty Facts and Stats," Global Issues, January 7, 2013, http:// www.globalissues.org/article/26/poverty-facts-and-stats.
5. http://www.callandresponse.com/about.html (link discontinued).
6. "Millennium Development Goals: Eradicate Extreme Poverty and Hunger," UNICEF, http://www.unicef.org/mdg/poverty.html (accessed March 19, 2014).
7. http://www.callandresponse.com/about.html (link discontinued).

8. "Modern Slavery Statistics," Abolition Media, http://abolitionmedia.org/about-us/modern-slavery-statistics (accessed March 19, 2014).

9. "The State of the World's Children 2006: Who are the Invisible?" UNICEF, http://www.unicef.org/sowc06/press/who.php (accessed March 19, 2014).

10. http://www.callandresponse.com/about.html (link discontinued).

11. Gustavo Capdevila, "Human Rights: More Than 100 Million Homeless Worldwide," Inter Press Service, March 30, 2005, http://www.ipsnews.net/2005/03/human-rights-more-than-100-million-homeless-worldwide/.

12. "Progress on Drinking Water and Sanitation: 2012 Update," UNICEF, http://www.unicef.org/media/files/JMPreport2012.pdf.

13. Pat Franklin, "Down the Drain," *Waste Management World* (May–June 2006), 62.

14. John de Graaf, David Wann, Thomas Naylor, *Affluenza: The All-Consuming Epidemic* (San Francisco: Berrett-Koehler, 2002), 87.

15. "Child Labour," Free the Children, http://www.freethechildren.com/get-involved/we-youth/resources/issues-backgrounder/ (accessed March 19, 2014).

16. Lyndsey Layton, "National Public High School Graduation Rates at a Four-Decade High," *Washington Post*, January 21, 2013, http://www.washingtonpost.com/local/education/national-high-school-graduation-rates-at-a-four-decade-high/2013/01/21/012cd7da-63e7-11e2-85f5-a8a9228e55e7_story.html.

17. "Social and Economic Injustice," World Centric, http://worldcentric.org/conscious-living/social-and-economic-injustice (accessed March 25, 2014).

18. "Obesity and Overweight," Centers for Disease Control and Prevention, http://www.cdc.gov/nchs/fastats/overwt.htm (accessed March 25, 2014).

19. Glenn Kessler, "U.S. Oil Resources," *Washington Post*, March 15, 2012, http://www.washingtonpost.com/blogs/fact-checker/post/us-oil-resources-president-obamas-non-sequitur-facts/2012/03/14/gIQApP14CS_blog.html.

20. "Frequently Asked Questions," U.S. Energy Information Administration, November 15, 2012, August 25, 2013, http://www.eia.gov/tools/faqs/faq.cfm?id=33&t=6.

21. Kenneth Rapoza, "Within Four Years, China to Consume More Oil than U.S.," Forbes, http://www.forbes.com/sites/kenrapoza/2013/08/25/within-four-years-china-to-consume-more-oil-than-u-s/.

22. Ali Abunimah, "The Media's Deadly Spin on Iraq," in *Iraq Under Siege*, ed. Anthony Arnove (Cambridge, MA: South End Press, 2002), 96.

23. George H. W. Bush, quoted in Jack Beatty, "Playing Politics with the Planet," *Atlantic Unbound* (April 14, 1999), http://www.theatlantic.com/unbound/polipro/pp9904.htm.

"NAME IT AND CLAIM IT" (AND I'LL SHAME IT)

1. "Weblog: Joel Osteen vs. Rick Warren on Prosperity Gospel," comp.
   Ted Olson, *Christianity Today*, September 14, 2006, http://www
   .christianitytoday.com/ct/2006/septemberweb-only/137-41.0.html.
2. Gloria Copeland, *God's Will is Prosperity* (Tulsa, OK: Harrison House,
   1987), 17.
3. Creflo Dollar, quoted in "Creflo Dollar, a Name that Has a Ring to It!"
   Let Us Reason, http://www.letusreason.org/Wf45.htm (accessed March 25,
   2014).
4. Rick Warren, quoted in David Van Biema and Jeff Chu, "Does God Want
   You to Be Rich?" *Time Magazine*, September 10, 2006, http://www.time
   .com/time/magazine/article/0,9171,1533448,00.html.
5. Colin Powell, quoted in "Powell Sees Eradicating Poverty as Real Fight
   against Terrorism," Kyodo News International, December 29, 2004.

GIVING THE GOOD STATS SOME PLAY

1. "Index of Global Philanthropy and Remittances 2013," Hudson
   Institute: The Center for Global Prosperity, http://www.hudson
   .org/content/researchattachments/attachment/1229/2013_indexof_global
   _philanthropyand_remittances.pdf.
2. "Index of Global Philanthropy and Remittances 2013," Hudson
   Institute: The Center for Global Prosperity, http://www.hudson.org
   /content/researchattachments/attachment/1229/2013_indexof_global
   _philanthropyand_remittances.pdf.
3. "Cost of National Security," National Priorities Project, http://national
   priorities.org/cost-of/ (accessed March 25, 2014).
4. Robert F. Kennedy, address on the Day of Affirmation: "It Is from the
   Numberless," University of Capetown, South Africa, June 6, 1966.
5. Proverbs 29:7.

BRANDON'S TAKE

1. Donna Bordelon Alder, "How to Encourage Your Pastor's Wife,"
   http://www.parsonage.org/articles/married/A000000065.cfm.

PHASE TWO: THE HORROR OF ACTUALLY CHANGING
TEACHING AN OLD DOG NEW TRICKS

1. Matthew 9:17.
2. Matthew 13:52.
3. Mark 1:27.
4. Romans 6:4.

5. Romans 7:6.
6. Galatians 6:15.
7. Ephesians 4:23.
8. Dictionary.com, s.v. "new," http://dictionary.reference.com/browse/new?s=t.
9. John 6:48, 53.

DESIRING, DOING, AND REMEMBERING

1. *Dodgeball: A True Underdog Story*, directed by Rawson Marshall Thurber (Los Angeles: Twentieth Century-Fox Film, 2004).
2. Luke 22:22.
3. John 10:18.
4. John 10:18.
5. Brian McLaren, *The Secret Message of Jesus* (Nashville: Thomas Nelson, 2006), 70.

BECOMING A LOWLIFE

1. *Back to the Future*, directed by Robert Zemeckis (Universal City, CA: Amblin Entertainment, 1985).
2. Richard Rohr, *Simplicity* (New York: Crossroad, 2003), 56–57.

"GET OFF YOUR HIGH HORSE"—JESUS

1. Shane Claiborne, *The Irresistible Revolution* (Grand Rapids, MI: Zondervan, 2006), 127.

GREAT

1. Søren Kierkegaard, *Provocations: Spiritual Writings of Kierkegaard*, ed. Charles E. Moore (Farmington, PA: Plough, 2002), 201.
2. Richard Rohr, *Simplicity* (New York: Crossroad, 2003), 144.

PHASE THREE: GETTING OUT THERE
DON'T KNOW IF WE'RE COMING OR GOING

1. "Twentysomethings Struggle to Find Their Place in Christian Churches," The Barna Group, September 24, 2003, https://www.barna.org/barna -update/article/5-barna-update/127-twentysomethings-struggle-to-find -their-place-in-christian-churches#.UytvdNy4mlI.
2. "Most Twentysomethings Put Christianity on the Shelf Following Spiritually Active Teen Years," The Barna Group, September 11, 2006, https://www.barna.org/barna-update/article/16-teensnext-gen/147-most -twentysomethings-put-christianity-on-the-shelf-following-spiritually -active-teen-years#.Uytwm9y4mlI.

3. The Barna Group, March 20, 2006, http://www.barna.org/barna-update/5-barna-update/158-spirituality-may-be-hot-in-america-but-76-million-adults-never-attend-church.

4. Tom Clegg and Warren Bird, *Lost in America* (Loveland, CO: Group, 2001), 27.

5. The Barna Group, http://www.barna.org/Flexpage.aspx?page=resource& resourceID=53 (link discontinued).

6. Clegg and Bird, 29.

7. Dr. Thom Rainer, quoted in Rebecca Barnes and Lindy Lowry, "Special Report: The American Church in Crisis," *Outreach Magazine*, May/June 2006, http://www.crossconnection.net/wp-content/uploads/2011/10/american_church_in_crisis.pdf.

8. Dr. Thom Rainer, "Ten Predictions for the Church by 2010 (Part I)," *Church Central*, December 27, 2002, http://www.churchcentral.com/article/536/Ten-Predictions-for-the-Church-by-2010-Part-I.

9. Clegg and Bird, 57–58.

10. Hugh Halter and Matt Smay, *The Tangible Kingdom* (San Francisco: Jossey-Bass, 2008), 9–10.

LAST BUT NOT LEAST

1. Shane Claiborne, *The Irresistible Revolution* (Grand Rapids, MI: Zondervan, 2006), 79.

POOR PEOPLE

1. Richard Rohr, *Simplicity* (New York: Crossroad, 2003).

NEW

1. Gerard Manley Hopkins, *Poems of Gerard Manley Hopkins*, "As Kingfishers Catch Fire" (New York: Digireads.com, 2010), 43.

2. Richard Rohr, *Simplicity* (New York: Crossroad, 2003), 57.

PHASE FOUR: FINDING YOUR TRIBE
ON A NEED-TO-KNOW BASIS

1. Dr. James Dobson, *When God Doesn't Make Sense* (Carol Stream, IL: Tyndale, 1993), 172.

FREE

1. B. T. Roberts, "Free Churches," *The Earnest Christian* (January 1860), quoted in Russell E. Richey, Kenneth E. Rowe, and Jean Miller Schmidt, *The Methodist Experience in America*, vol. 2 (Nashville: Abingdon Press, 2000), 297–298.

2. B. T. Roberts, "Object and Scope of This Magazine," *The Earnest Christian*, quoted in Howard A Snyder, *Popular Saints* (Grand Rapids: Eerdmans, 2006), 547.
3. B. T. Roberts, "Object and Scope of This Magazine," 546.

IGNORANCE IS NOT BLISS
1. Jeremiah 17:9.
2. Hugh Halter and Matt Smay, *The Tangible Kingdom* (San Francisco: Jossey-Bass, 2008), 125.

A MODERN MESS
1. Mary E. DeMuth, *Authentic Parenting in a Postmodern Culture* (Eugene, OR: Harvest House, 2007), 22–23.
2. Halter and Smay, *The Tangible Kingdom* (San Francisco: Jossey-Bass, 2008), 61–75; DeMuth, 22–23.

"TURN AND FACE THE STRANGE CH-CH-CHANGES"
1. Halter and Smay, *The Tangible Kingdom* (San Francisco: Jossey-Bass, 2008), 63.
2. DeMuth, *Authentic Parenting in a Postmodern Culture* (Eugene, OR: Harvest House, 2007), 24–25.
3. DeMuth, 24–27.
4. DeMuth, 27.

MISSION POSSIBLE
1. Shane Claiborne, *The Irresistible Revolution* (Grand Rapids, MI: Zondervan, 2006), 24.

PHASE FIVE: SENT
MISSION . . . AL?
1. Daryl R. Eldridge, "Reaching Your Unchurched Community the New Testament Way," LifeWay, http://www.lifeway.com/Article/ministry -evangelism-Reaching-Your-Unchurched-Community-the-New-Testament -Way (accessed April 3, 2014).
2. Ed Stetzer and David Putman, *Breaking the Missional Code* (Nashville: Broadman & Holman, 2006), 44.
3. Stetzer and Putman, 33.

OFFERING A TANGIBLE KINGDOM
1. Hugh Halter and Matt Smay, *The Tangible Kingdom* (San Francisco: Jossey-Bass, 2008), 30.

2. Halter and Smay, 42.
3. Halter and Smay, 46.

RIGHT TO REMAIN SILENT
1. John 1:12.
2. Galatians 4:4-7.
3. Revelation 22:14.
4. Revelation 3:21.
5. Romans 6:22.
6. Colossians 2:8.
7. Matthew Henry, *Matthew Henry's Commentary on the Whole Bible: Acts to Revelation*, vol. 6, http://www.ccel.org/ccel/henry/mhc6.pdf.

CHANGELINGS
1. Albert Barnes, *Notes Explanatory and Practical, on the First Epistle of Paul to the Corinthians* (New York: Harper & Brothers, 1841), 182.

IN THE CITY, FOR THE CITY
1. Martin Luther King Jr., quoted in Clayborne Carson and Kris Shepard, eds., *A Call to Conscience* (New York: Warner Books, 2001), 56.

About the Author

Jen happily lives in Austin, Texas, where the city motto is "Keep Austin Weird." (She is certainly doing her part.) Jen and her husband, Brandon, have five kids—Gavin, Sydney, Caleb, Ben, and Remy. They lead Austin New Church, a faith community obsessed with bringing justice and restoration to the city and the world.

Jen has written nine books and Bible studies, including bestseller *7: An Experimental Mutiny Against Excess.* She travels all over the United States teaching at conferences. To read her highly trafficked blog, see her travel schedule, or learn more about her ministry, go to www.jenhatmaker.com for more details.